UNDER
HIS
BANNER

VINSON SYNAN

UNDER HIS BANNER

gift publications

Costa Mesa, California

©Copyright, 1992 by Vinson Synan
Published by Gift Publications
Costa Mesa, California 92626

ISBN # 0-86595-019-9

Cover and graphics: Cornell Morton

Printed in the United States of America.

Dedicated to
DEMOS SHAKARIAN

For his prophetic leadership in founding and leading Full Gospel Business Men's Fellowship International, thereby raising up a worldwide army of Spirit-filled lay witnesses to Jesus Christ.

"Behold, I have given him for a witness to the people, a leader and commander to the people.

"Behold, thou shalt call a nation that thou knowest not, and nations that knew not thee shall run unto thee because of the Lord thy God, and for the Holy One of Israel: for he hath glorified thee."—*Isaiah 55:4-5*

CONTENTS

Foreword 7

His Banner Over Me Is Love 11

Demos 17

First Efforts 29

The Birth Of The Fellowship 43

A Nationwide Movement 59

An International Movement 71

FGBMFI—An Ecumenical Force 87

On The Heights 101

The Men Of The Fellowship 119

The Testimonies 141

The Fellowship At Forty 153

Appendix 165

CONTENTS

FOREWORD

God has brought our Fellowship through a lot the past forty years. I look back with thanksgiving at highlights of His divine direction and protection in each of the last four decades.

The 1950's brought the birth of the Fellowship. The Lord had burdened my heart to reach laymen for Christ. After a shaky beginning, we watched the Spirit of God use Full Gospel Business Men's Fellowship, in cooperation with the nation's leading healing evangelists, to awaken within Christendom a new vision and understanding of God's power to heal. As the decade came to a close FGBMFI was at the crest of the charismatic wave that was sweeping thousands from the historic churches into the experience of the baptism in the Holy Spirit.

In the heart of the 1960's the Fellowship moved from a part-time effort in spreading the gospel to other parts of the world to an all-out international blitz as a result of our London airlift. Our businessmen shared testimonies all over Europe. Hundreds of people from beatniks to barristers were saved and filled with the Holy Spirit. The impact of these meetings spread throughout Europe and continues worldwide today as FGBMFI ministers in 120 countries of the world.

Late in 1960, under the influence of Ray Bullard and other Full Gospel Businessmen, students and faculty at Notre Dame University in South Bend, Indiana began to receive the baptism in the Holy Spirit. This contributed a vital part to the growth of the Catholic Charismatic Renewal that has influenced the lives of more than 70 million Catholics.

1970 was highlighted by our television ministry, "Good News". Starting small it wasn't long until we were in hundreds of markets and soon chapters around the world were sponsoring a growing international ministry. The tremendous response to our regular telecast and the additional impact of our TV specials gave us spiritual response beyond our wildest imagination.

Later in 1970 millions of people became acquainted with the Fellowship through my book *The Happiest People On Earth*. It has been translated into more than twenty-five languages.

1980 found us in a new headquarters building. This building, designed to be the international home of the Fellowship, is one of the most attractive and well-planned Christian office buildings in America.

The latter part of the 1980's presented some problems for our Fellowship. However the Lord delivered us through the difficulties and brought us to the brink of the greatest spiritual revival the world will ever know.

Launching into the decade of the nineties we are awaiting the mighty outpouring of His Spirit. Rejoice with us in what the past has wrought and look forward with us to revival just ahead.

I want to thank Dr. Vinson Synan for the wonderful job he has done on this fortieth anniversary history book. He has served as the General Secretary and later as Assistant General Superintendent of the Pentecostal Holiness denomination. He is a recognized historian with a Ph.D. in history from the University of Georgia. He has written some ten books, and served as founder and president of the Society for Pentecostal Studies. He serves as a member of the American and International

Lausanne Committees and the Executive Committee of the International Charismatic Consultation on World Evangelization. He is Chairman of the North American Renewal Services Committee and as such chaired the Great Congresses in New Orleans and Indianapolis.

It is indeed an honor for us in FGBMFI to have him edit our fortieth anniversary history book.

Demos Shakarian

Chapter One

HIS BANNER OVER ME IS LOVE

He brought me to His banqueting table, His banner over me is love.—Song of Solomon 2:4 (popular chorus at FGBMFI dinners)

Full Gospel Business Men's Fellowship International (FGBMFI) is perhaps the largest and most important Christian laymen's organization in the United States and the world. Begun in 1951 in a Los Angeles cafeteria by Demos Shakarian, an Armenian-American dairyman, it had grown by the late 1980's to encompass over 3,000 chapters in 117 nations of the world. Of these, 1,700 were in the United States claiming 45,000 full members. Monthly attendance figures, however, vastly outstripped membership statistics. In America no less than 500,000 persons attended monthly meetings, while world attendance totaled over 1,000,000 persons.[1]

Although the Fellowship was ecumenical from the beginning, attracting members from all churches of Christendom, it began essentially as a Pentecostal parachurch organization which unabashedly promoted pentecostal practices such as speaking in tongues and divine healing to all who came, regardless of ecclesiastical or theological background. Beginning among Classical Pentecostals, the Fellowship welcomed each new wave of

11

Pentecostalism as the movement swept through the churches of Protestantism and even into the Roman Catholic church.

That an organization of this magnitude has escaped the attention of the academic world is indeed a mystery. As of 1990, not one master's thesis or doctoral dissertation had chronicled the history of this burgeoning organization. Neither has any serious historian or publisher attempted to examine the role of FGBMFI in the development of the charismatic movement in the mainline churches. The best known source is Demos Shakarian's own autobiography entitled *The Happiest People on Earth: The Long Awaited Personal Story of Demos Shakarian as Told to John And Elizabeth Sherrill* (1975). By 1990 this book had sold over 1,000,000 copies and had been translated into 25 languages. Until now, *The Happiest People on Earth,* has been the major and most reliable source of information about the history of the Fellowship. First published in 1976, it has served as an indispensable guide for untold thousands who were attracted to the Fellowship. But much has happened since 1976 which should now be included in the story.[2]

This book is a first attempt to piece together the main strands of the FGBMFI story during its entire forty-year history. This is a descriptive history and makes no pretense at being the final definitive and critical work on the history of the Fellowship. Unquestionably, the story of FGBMFI is a history that needs to be written because of the incredible impact the organization has had on untold thousands of lives. It is a story that could happen only in America, and then only in a particular time of American religious life. It is a story so unique that it is unlikely to be repeated in this or any other century.

Its very name, "Full Gospel", marked it as a part of the fast-growing Pentecostal movement which had beginnings in turn-of-the-century America. But by the end of the century Pentecostalism had spread to all parts of the globe claiming over 400,000,000 persons around the world by the time Full Gospel Business Men's Fellowship International launched its fortieth anniversary celebration in 1992. Many people think that Full Gospel played an important role in that growth. The earliest contribution of FGBMFI was to bring the healing evangelists to the attention of the non-pentecostal world. As Walter Hollenweger affirmed, "Full Gospel Business Men can claim credit for having gained a hearing for the healing evangelists in the non-pentecostal churches."[3]

It also opened the door for Pentecostalism to enter the mainline churches through the charismatic movement that flourished after 1960. The Fellowship brought the pentecostal experience to a new generation of middle-class businessmen, many of whom would never have stepped into a pentecostal church. In the ballroom gatherings of the Fellowship, people from all church traditions from Baptists to Roman Catholics received Spirit-filled ministry which they likely would never have found elsewhere. As historian David Harrell said, "The fantastic growth of the Fellowship marked the acceptance of charismatic religion by thousands of successful middle-class people" who were attracted by the neutral non-ecclesiastical surroundings of Full Gospel dinner meetings.[4]

Full Gospel meetings provided a setting where the economically successful could gather together and praise the Lord for prosperity as well as for spiritual and physical healing. At first the combination of the words "Full Gospel" and "Businessman" seemed like a contradiction in terms to those who saw pentecostals as deprived and ignorant members of the disinherited underclass. But the Fellowship succeeded in presenting a new image for tongue speakers, that of well-to-do Christians who could do as well in business and the professions as most anybody else. This change in self-image prompted such people as Glenn Randall, a retired professor at North Carolina State University and founder of the Raleigh chapter, to proudly drive his car around town with "FGBMFI" emblazoned on his license plate.[5]

In 1992, FGBMFI began a year-long fortieth anniversary celebration of ministry around the world. In biblical days, forty years was a most significant anniversary. It meant at the least the ending of one generation and the beginning of the next. It is significant that the Fellowship was able to celebrate its fortieth year with its founder, Demos Shakarian, still in office and directing the affairs of the organization. This is in itself highly unusual and points to the durability not only of the founder, but of the movement he began.[6]

There are many reasons why I wanted to write this book. The main one was that my life was irrevocably changed in 1970 when I attended a Full Gospel regional convention in Charlotte, North Carolina. Although I had met Demos Shakarian in 1954 when he spoke at Emmanuel College, where I was enrolled as a college freshman, I was deeply moved in the Charlotte meeting when for the first time I saw Baptists, Methodists, and Presbyterians enjoying the blessings that we Pentecostals had enjoyed in our churches for decades. Here for the first time I saw mainline Christians prophesy, speak in tongues, and pray for the sick.

It also was a personal turning point for me when I saw a Lutheran pastor receive the Pentecostal experience and speak in a tongue which seemed to be a middle-eastern language. The fact that this happened in a hotel room also seemed incredible to me at the time. This was my first exposure to the pentecostal renewal in the mainline Protestant churches. It was two years later that I first came in contact with the Catholic Charismatic

Renewal at Notre Dame University in South Bend, Indiana.

For me, Full Gospel Business Men's Fellowship International was the first instrument that helped me see the wider work of the Holy Spirit moving in and through the entire Body of Christ.[7]

For this I will be eternally grateful.

1. *The emphasis on the importance of the laity may be seen in the large number of books written on lay movements in this century. Modern views on Catholic laity can be found in Yves Congar's* Lay People in the Church; A Study for a Theology of the Laity. *Translated by Donald Attwater (Westminster, Maryland: Newman Press, 1965); on mainline protestantism in Georgia Harkness'* The Church and its Laity *(New York: Abingdon Press, 1962); on evangelicals in Ralph D. Bucy's* The New Laity; Between Church and the World *(Waco, Texas: Word Books, 1976). Major lay organizations that preceded FGBMFI included the Young Men's Christian Association (YMCA) founded in 1840 and the Gideons founded in 1899. A twentieth century forerunner was the Christian Business Men's Committee International which was founded in 1930 and is now headquartered in Chattanooga, Tennessee. For an example of CBMC literature, see David R. Enlow,* Men Made New *(Grand Rapids: Zondervan, 1964).*

2. *Among the few published sources for FGBMFI are: John Sherrill's,* The Happiest People on Earth; The Long-Awaited Personal Story of Demos Shakarian as told to John and Elizabeth Sherrill *(Lincoln, Virginia: Chosen Books, 1975); Steve Durasoff's* Bright Wind of the Spirit; Pentecostalism Today *(Englewood Cliffs, N.J.: Prentice-Hall, 1972); and David Edwin Harrell's* All Things Are Possible; The Healing and Charismatic Movements in Modern America *(Bloomington, Indiana: The University of Indiana Press, 1975); Brian Bird, "The Legacy of Demos Shakarian,"* Charisma, *June, 1986, 21-25; and James Zeigler's "Full Gospel Business Men's Fellowship International (FGBMFI)" in the* Dictionary of Pentecostal and Charismatic Movements, *edited by Stanley M. Burgess, Gary McGee, and Patrick H. Alexander (Grand Rapids, Michigan: Zondervan Publishing House, 1988), 321-322.*

3. *Major recent sources on Pentecostalism include: Donald Dayton,* Theological Roots of Pentecostalism *(Metuchen, N.J.: Scarecrow Press, 1987); Robert Mapes Anderson's* Vision of the Disinherited *(New York: Oxford University Press, 1979); Vinson Synan,* The Holiness Pentecostal Movement in the United States *(Grand Rapids, Michigan: Wm. E. Eerdmans, 1972); Edith Blumhofer,* The Assemblies of God; A Chapter in the Story of American Pentecostalism, *2 Vols. (Springfield, Missouri:*

Gospel Publishing House, 1989); and James R. Goff, Fields White Unto Harvest; Charles Fox Parham and the Missionary Origins of Pentecostalism *(Fayetteville, Arkansas: The University of Arkansas Press, 1990).*

4. Concise sources for the Charismatic Movement in the mainline churches include: Kilian McDonnell, Charismatic Movement and the Churches *(New York: the Seabury Press, 1976); Michael Harper,* As At the Beginning; The Twentieth Century Pentecostal Revival *(London: Hodder & Staughton, 1965); also see Vinson Synan's,* In the Latter Days *(Ann Arbor, Michigan, Servant Books, 1984, 1991); and* The Twentieth Century Pentecostal Explosion *(Altamonte Springs, Florida: Creation House, 1987). Official church documents relating to the renewal may be found in Kilian McDonnel's* Presence, Power, Praise; Documents on the Charismatic Renewal, *3 vols. (Collegeville, Minnesota: Liturgical Press, 1980). A comprehensive guide to the literature of the movement can be found in Charles Jones'* The Charismatic Movement; A Guide to the Study of Neo-Pentecostalism *(Metuchen, New Jersey: ATLA-Scarecrow Press, 1992) 2 vols.*

5. Glenn O. Randall, "Winter Wonderland." Voice, *December 1973, pp. 5-35.*

6. Major primary sources for the FGBMFI story include: the issues of Full Gospel Business Men's *Voice which have appeared monthly since February of 1953 (hereafter cited as* Voice). *Also Jerry Jensen* The Shakarian Story, *(Los Angeles: FGBMFI publication, 1964) and his "How God Raised up Our Fellowship," in* Voice, January, 1958. *Also two transcribed personal interviews with the author and Demos Shakarian on October 5, 1987 and February 2, 1988.*

7. See Vinson Synan (interview) "Winning the World." Voice, *June, 1987, pp. 2-11.*

Chapter Two

DEMOS

"How was it possible, we kept asking ourselves, that this shy, inarticulate man with the slow gentle smile, a man who never seems to be in a hurry, never seems to know today where he'll be tomorrow, could be having such an impact on millions of people? We decided to find out."
—*John and Elizabeth Sherrill, 1976*

If it is true, as has often been said, "that an institution is but the lengthened shadow of one man," then for Full Gospel Business Men's Fellowship International, that man is Demos Shakarian. The son of Armenian immigrants to California who made their living as dairy farmers, Shakarian has taken his place as one of the most important lay leaders in Christian history.

The story of FGBMFI is forever intertwined with the biography of this unassuming but determined Californian whose prophetic vision helped fuel one of the most important renewal movements of modern times.

PENTECOSTAL ROOTS

The roots of Full Gospel Business Men's Fellowship International can be traced to two small congregations in Los Angeles soon after the turn of the century. The first was the well-known Azusa Street Mission, which brought the fledgling Pentecostal movement to the attention of the religious world. Under the leadership of William J. Seymour, a black pastor from Louisiana, the Azusa mission in the years 1906-1909 became the single most important center for the spread of the movement. Pentecostalism had begun in 1901 in Topeka, Kansas under Charles F. Parham, a former Methodist minister who insisted that speaking in other tongues was the "initial evidence" of a post-conversion experience called "the baptism in the Holy Spirit."[1]

The other congregation was a small church meeting in a home on Boston Street in Los Angeles. This house church served a group of Armenian immigrants who had arrived in California in 1905 to escape persecution from the Turks in Armenia. Among the Armenians who attended the church was Demos Shakarian (grandfather of the founder of FGBMFI) and his son Isaac. The younger Shakarian made a living by selling vegetables on the streets of Los Angeles.

One day Demos and his cousin, Magardich Mushegan, walked by the Azusa Street Mission near San Pedro Avenue in downtown Los Angeles and were immediately attracted by the powerful service which included speaking in tongues, prophecies, and healing in answer to prayer. As they entered the church, which was led by the African-American pastor, William J. Seymour, they immediately recognized that the worship was similar to their own Armenian form of spiritual worship. Shortly thereafter, the Armenian church on Boston Street became a full fledged Pentecostal congregation, and in time moved to a new church building on Gless Street.[2]

One of the youths raised in this church was Demos Shakarian, the firstborn son of Isaac Shakarian. Demos, who was named for his grandfather, was born on July 21, 1913 in Downey, California in a wooden plank house. By the time Demos was born, the Shakarian family had prospered after his father had entered the dairy business.[3]

ARMENIAN ROOTS

The Shakarian family came to America from Armenia, a country which prides itself in claiming to be the first officially Christian nation in the world. Although for centuries an independent nation, Armenia was for most of the twentieth century a republic of the USSR. Always influenced by Russia, Armenia had experienced developments in its religious life that paralleled those of Russia. Although dominated by the Orthodox Church, both Russia and Armenia had seen the rise of many dissident Christian sects in recent centuries. Some of these groups were radical ecstatic movements that began in reaction to the strict liturgical tradition of orthodoxy. Among these were the Khlysty of the 18th Century and the Molokans of the 19th Century. Both of these movements disdained the regular liturgies of the church and opted for an emotionally-charged style of worship.[4]

While the Khlysty were known for their frenetic dances which often ended with the participants falling on the floor in spiritual and physical exhaustion, the Molokans were known for their more restrained circle dances "in the Spirit" which often included prophecies and spiritual ecstasies. During the 1800's the Khlysty movement declined while the Molokans flourished, spreading throughout Russia and neighboring countries. Later such Protestant sects as the Presbyterians and Baptists entered Russia, attracting Molokans to their more sedate services. The Baptists, in particular, succeeded in winning tens of thousands of Molokans to their church.[5]

While many Armenians had been won to the Presbyterian church, including the Shakarian family, thousands of Russians left Orthodoxy to join the ranks of the fast-growing Molokan sect. The central feature of Molokan worship was the prayer meeting which was conducted with everyone standing in a circle praying for the expected descent of the Holy Spirit.

A more expressive faction of the Molokans was also known as the "Priguny" (jumpers) because many would jump and shout when the Spirit fell. All this was done without an ordained clergy or written forms of worship. Often these Christians would also prophesy about future events as they were inspired by the Holy Spirit.[6]

In 1900, a group of Molokans from Russia crossed the border into Armenia and were received by the Presbyterians and others as brothers and sisters in Christ. As the result of a "word of knowledge" about a missing cow's head, the Shakarian family accepted the Molokan respect for prophecy. Although there is no evidence that these Russian Christians were "classical pentecostals" in the twentieth-century sense of the word, they were clearly ecstatics who could well be classified as "pre-pentecostals."[7]

The Shakarian family came from the city of Kara Kala, located in the foothills of Mount Ararat near where Noah's ark rested, a region dangerously close to Moslem Turkey. For centuries there had been occasional massacres of the Christian Armenians whom the Turks considered to be "infidels". It was from this background that a striking prophecy was given in 1853 which ultimately caused the Shakarian family to immigrate to the United States. The written prophecy, which was given by an eleven-year-old boy by the name of Efrim, warned the citizens of Kara Kala to flee to a nation in the West where they would be safe from harm. They were told to journey all the way to the west coast of America, a land they had never seen. Those who remained, the prophecy warned, would be murdered by the Turks.[8]

Many Armenians in Kara Kala ignored the warnings of the "boy prophet" and stayed in Armenia where they were indeed massacred by the Turks in 1914. The Shakarians and many others, however, were convinced that the prophecy was from the Lord and soon made preparations to journey to the west. After selling their cherished land that had been in the family for generations, the Shakarians left for America in 1905 and joined several thousand other Russians and Armenians in the bustling city of Los Angeles, California.[9]

THE SHAKARIANS IN LOS ANGELES

In 1905, records reveal that no less than 3,200 Russians were already living in the city, 3,000 of whom belonged to the Molokan sect. The remaining 200 were from the Russian Orthodox Church. That the Molokans were clearly pre-pentecostals was evident by their style of worship. According to Lillian Sokoloff, a student of Russian immigration to Los Angeles.[10]

Additionally, the Molokans practiced an ascetic style of personal holiness which paralleled similar "holiness" movements in America. Among other things, they prohibited the use of alcohol or tobacco, and like the Orthodox Jews, abstained from eating pork.[11] When the Shakarians were exposed to the pentecostal style of worship at Azusa Street, immediately they recognized the similarities between the Pentecostals and their own religious tradition. Throughout the Armenian quarter of Los Angeles, the faithful worshiped in their homes, simple buildings that were usually overcrowded with newly-arrived immigrants from overseas. The Shakarian family home on Boston Avenue was one such home that on Sundays became a church.[12]

Eventually the Armenian congregation built a church on Gless Street and moved their worship services out of the home on Boston Avenue. It was a small sanctuary, 30 by 60 feet, furnished with only a table and oriental rug on the front wall and backless pews which could be shoved against the walls "when the joy of the Lord moved the congregation to dance in the Spirit."[13]

In the new world of Los Angeles, the Shakarian family life centered on their home, their church, and their work. The elder Demos Shakarian first made a living building railroads near Las Vegas where he worked alongside Chinese coolies in the stifling heat of the American West. His son, Isaac, made the best living he could by working in a harness factory. A great tragedy struck the family when the elder Demos died suddenly while working on the railroads. At this sad news, the 14-year-old Isaac, now the breadwinner for the family, forsook the factory to work a ten-acre farm from which he could sell vegetables off a wagon in downtown Los Angeles. From truck farming, he later turned to raising cattle and selling milk to the citizens of the city. Starting with only three cows, he was able through dedication and hard work to eventually build the largest dairy herd in the United States, which ultimately reached a grand total of 5,000 animals.[14]

Following family tradition, young Demos worked with his father on the dairy ranch as well as assisting him in the Armenian church, where his father served as an important elder. In time Demos became a youth leader in the Church. As a true pentecostal, Demos also was "baptized in the Holy Spirit" and spoke in tongues in 1926 when he was 13 years old. This was to be a life-changing experience for the young boy and crucial to his later vision for Spirit-filled laymen who would exercise the gifts of the Spirit. When he received "the Baptism" he was sitting on the rear bench of the little church. Suddenly he felt as if he could not move a muscle, then:

> "My jaw began to shake as if I were shivering with cold...muscles in the back of my throat tightened. I had a sudden yearning to tell Jesus that I loved Him, but when I opened my mouth to say so, out came words I couldn't understand. I knew they were not Armenian, or Spanish, or English, but they poured out of me as though I had been speaking them all my life."[15]

At the same time he received the baptism in the Holy Spirit, Shakarian testified to having been healed of partial deafness which had plagued him for most of his life. After these events he felt called to share these pentecostal blessings with everyone he met. Although he greatly desired to be used of God, Demos never felt that he had been endowed with prophetic gifts. Never did he claim to be called into the ministry. Mostly he was content to serve as a layman and promote others in whom he saw such gifts operating.

A SPIRIT-FILLED LAYMAN

In 1932 Demos felt attracted to a pretty young Armenian girl in the church by the name of Rose Gabrielian. He soon desired desperately to court and marry her, but he was prevented from talking to her by the strict customs of the Armenian culture. According to tradition, marriages were arranged by the parents. At long last, when he was permitted to talk to her, Demos' first words were "Rose, I know God wants us together." Her tearful response was, "All my life I have prayed that the man I married would say those words to me first of all." It was indeed a marriage made in heaven. The wedding took place before 500 guests on August 6, 1933 in the church on Gless Street following the ancient Armenian wedding ceremony conducted by Pastor Perumean. Afterwards, the young Shakarians dedicated their home, their future family, and their lives to the Lord.[16]

By the time Demos was married, the Shakarian dairy herd was the largest in California. His wife shared his interest in spiritual matters and was later to play an important role in the development of the Full Gospel Business Men's Fellowship. In time, the couple was blessed with three children, Richard, Geraldine, and Stephen. As the children grew, the Shakarian family business prospered greatly. Not only did Isaac and Demos run a large dairy, they also branched out into a meat packing plant as well as operating a fleet of 400 trucks that delivered milk from their dairy to stores and businesses throughout California.[17]

The growth of the business and the prosperity that followed made their lives easier but did nothing to quench the spiritual ardor of the young couple. Their lives were as much as ever centered around their church, their family, and the work of the Lord. In 1937 their lives were deeply influenced by the sudden utterance of several personal prophecies given to them by a house painter friend named Milton Hansen. One night in a home prayer meeting, Hansen raised his hands, began to shake, and predicted that Shakarian would "speak of holy matters with heads of state around the world." This confirmed in Shakarian's spirit a much earlier prophecy given by the Russian prophet at the time Armenian Christians were warned to flee to the United States. This prophecy stated that "I will cause your seed to be a blessing to the nations."[18] All these prophecies were a bit puzzling to the Shakarians since they had never set foot outside of California in their lives.

Four years later, in 1941, an astounding miracle of divine healing convinced Shakarian that amazing healings could occur if Christians would only pray the "prayer of faith." This healing experience came after his sister Florence was seriously injured in an automobile accident. With her pelvis crushed and serious burns over her back, the doctors held out little hope for recovery.

Hearing that a healing evangelist, Charles R. Price, was preaching in nearby Maywood, California, Shakarian hurried to the tent to invite Price to pray for his sister. Despite exhaustion from preaching, Price agreed to go to the hospital to pray for the stricken girl. According to biographer Jim Zeigler, "Dr. Price laid hands on Shakarian's sister and as her body shook for twenty minutes under the power of God her shattered pelvis was healed. The next morning new X rays revealed a completely restored pelvis in place of the crushed and dislocated one of the day before."[19]

This healing made a lifetime impression on Shakarian, leading to his total support of the healing revival that swept across America and much of the world after World War II. The healing ministries of Oral Roberts, William Branham, and Tommy Hicks were to be crucial to the founding of Full Gospel Business Men's Fellowship after 1951 and to its growth thereafter. Because of the healing of his sister, Shakarian became a close friend of Price, a man who was to play an important part in forming his vision for the "layman's revival" after World War II.

The cumulative effect of these charismatic events in Shakarian's life, his baptism in the Holy Spirit evidenced by speaking in tongues, his own healing from deafness as well as the healing of his sister, and the prophecies of his future ministry, had a deeply moving effect on the young California businessman. Although he was not sure how all of this this would come about, he was convinced that he had been given a special mission in God's providence that ultimately would bless the world.

1. For succinct treatments of Parham and Seymour, see Burgess, et.al., Dictionary of Pentecostal and Charismatic Movements, *pp. 660-661 and 778-781. An excellent treatment of Parham's life is given in Goff's* Fields White Unto Harvest *while the story of Seymour's life is given in Douglas Nelson's* For Such a Time as This; The Story of Bishop William J. Seymour and the Azusa Street Revival *(unpublished Ph.D. Dissertation, University of Birmingham (U.I.), 1981).*

2. Sherrill, Happiest People On Earth, *pp. 23-24.*

3. Shakarian told and retold the story of the family background in Armenia and America in many sources including: The Happiest People on Earth, *pp. 13-30; and a series in* Voice *entitled "The Amazing Shakarian Story", (October 1953-Feb.-March 1954). The same story is told in Jerry Jensen's* The Shakarian Story *(Los Angeles: FGBMFI publication, 1964) pp. 3-14).*

4. For an excellent treatment of Russian ecstatic movements such as the Khlysty, the Molokans, and the Pentecostals see William C. Fletcher's Soviet Charismatics; The Pentecostals in the U.S.S.R. *(New York: Peter Lang Publishing Co., 1985), pp. 11-27; 27-149.*

5. Ibid., *pp. 11-21, 72, 107.*

6. For more on the Priguny see Ibid., *pp. 18; 22-25.*

7. See Happiest People On Earth, *pp. 16-19. Although Sherrill and Jensen speak of the Armenians as "Pentecostals," there is little evidence that these people spoke in tongues or considered glossolalia to be the "initial evidence" of baptism in the Holy Spirit. They could well fit David Barrett's category of "Pre-pentecostals" or "quasi-pentecostals" as described in his "The 20th Century Pentecostal/Charismatic Renewal in the Holy Spirit, With its Goal of World Evangelization" in the* International Bulletin of Missionary Research *(July 1988), pp. 2, 7.*

8. Sherrill, Happiest People On Earth, *pp. 19-21.*

9. Ibid., *pp. 21-23.*

10. Information on Russian immigrants to Los Angeles in 1905 as well as Molokan worship patterns may be found in Lillian Sokoloff's 1918 monograph entitled "The Russians in Los Angeles," Studies in Sociology, *No. 11, Vol. III, March 1918, pp. 1-15.*

11. Ibid., *p. 7.*

12. Shakarian-Synan interview, pp. 2-3. Sherrill, Happiest People On Earth, *p. 24.*

13. Ibid., *pp. 62-68, 117; Shakarian-Synan interview, October, 5, 1987, pp. 30-32. Also see "The Amazing Shakarian Story,"* Voice, *December, 1953, pp. 8-10.*

14. Shakarian-Synan interview, October 5, 1987; Durasoff, Bright Wind, *p. 145. Also see Jerry Jensen,* The Shakarian Story, *(Los Angeles,*

FGBMFI, 1964) pp. 23-27, and Sherrill, Happiest People On Earth, *pp. 28-30.*

15. *Sherrill,* Ibid., *pp. 35-37.*

16. *The story of the courtship and marriage, with the Armenian ceremony is given in Sherrill,* Happiest People On Earth, *pp. 40-47.*

17. *Synan-Shakarian interview, p.3. Also see Jensen* The Shakarian Story, *pp. 23-27.*

18. Ibid., *p.51; Shakarian-Synan interview, pp.30-32; also see "The Amazing Shakarian Story,"* Voice, *December, 1953, pp. 8-10.*

19. *Jim Zeigler, "Demos Shakarian" in Burgess, et. al.* Dictionary, *pp.781- 782. Also see Sherrill,* Happiest People On Earth, *pp. 64-71; and Jerry Jensen,* The Shakarian Story *(Los Angeles, FGBMFI, 1964), pp. 20-21.*

Chapter Three

FIRST EFFORTS

"I'm lucky, I've found my job. I'm a helper...My gift is to help other people do what they do best. I'll help you get together, help set up the meeting place, help you find speakers. What I'll get out of it is the joy of using the talent God gave me."—Demos Shakarian

The prophecies given to Shakarian by Hansen and Price began the process of fulfillment in 1940 when Shakarian attempted his first public preaching in a lot across from a Los Angeles public park. For some time, he and Rose had felt that they should try in some way to reach the masses of unbelievers who lived and worked around them. Demos was especially concerned about the men who worked for him who never said a word about God. This was in stark contrast to the Shakarian family where the Lord was the subject of almost every conversation.

About ten miles from Downey there was a large public park known as Lincoln Park. On Sundays as many as 4,000 persons would gather for recreation and picnics. The Shakarians had gone there over the years and wondered just how many of them knew Jesus as Saviour. One day Demos mentioned to Rose that he had seen a vision of himself speaking to masses of people from a platform. She finished the sentence..."in Lincoln Park." Thus began Demos' short-lived career as an itinerant evangelist. Unable to get permits to use the park, he was able to rent an adjacent lot where people in the park could hear him over loudspeakers.

On the first Sunday of June, 1940, after Rose and a trio of girls had sung several hymns, a fearful young Demos climbed to the platform to preach his first public sermon. One of his greatest fears was that some business acquaintance from the Kiwanis Club might see him and laugh at his efforts. To his surprise and relief, an acquaintance did see him, but instead of laughing, he came to the platform and with tears of repentance, surrendered his life to the Lord. This emboldened Shakarian to continue his preaching in the park. For three months, the Sunday afternoon meetings proceeded with up to ten persons converted in each meeting. A painful and unexpected source of criticism came from the Armenian church on Gless Street. Some of the elders thought it was "un-Armenian" for Demos to do such preaching in public.[1]

At the end of the summer, however, hundreds had gathered to hear Rose sing and Demos testify about the love of Jesus. This meeting revealed the fact that Shakarian, if not the greatest preacher around, was a man whose vision went far beyond his local church. Soon after the Lincoln Park meetings, he conceived of a plan to conduct a tent meeting sponsored by several local Pentecostal churches. Often Shakarian had been saddened by the seeming indifference that these churches showed to the unconverted people in the surrounding cities who never went inside the sanctuaries of the churches. He also felt that their petty denominational rivalries and lack of fellowship stunted their witness to the world.

Against the suspicions of the Armenian church elders, he and his father persuaded the elders to let him use a church-owned lot to conduct a tent crusade in the spring of 1941. With his cousin Harry Mushegan chosen as the evangelist, Demos set to work renting a tent and obtaining the necessary permits from the city to hold the crusade. At the time he was working tirelessly for the crusade, his new fertilizer business went bankrupt, the only business failure he was to experience during his lifetime.

The tent crusade lasted for six weeks and was notable for the ecumenical cooperation of the local Pentecostal churches. Equally amazing was the fact that the offerings received in the services more than paid for the costs of the meeting. The most far-reaching effect though, as Demos saw it, was the cooperation of the local pastors. As he explained:

> In order to make decisions about it (the crusade and its expenses), the pastor of the Foursquare Church telephoned the pastor of the Pentecostal Church of God. An elder of the Assemblies of God was seen having lunch with an elder of the Armenian Pentecostal church. And both of them actually walked through the door and sat down to worship with the Pentecostal Holiness congregation down the street...[2]

In this tent crusade, Shakarian was uniquely successful in uniting these churches in a manner unprecedented for the times. Not even in the heyday of the Aimee Semple McPherson crusades had local Pentecostal churches demonstrated such unity. The power of a unified witness across denominational lines was a lesson that Shakarian would never forget.

This vision for Pentecostal ecumenism had originally been impressed on Shakarian by evangelist Charles Price, who at this time served as Demos' spiritual mentor. It was Price's contention that the pentecostal churches constituted a "sleeping giant" that could shake the world if they could ever get together.

He was convinced that great crowds could be assembled if Pentecostals could be brought together in a spirit of unity rather than competition. It was Price who popularized the term "full gospel" as an umbrella term which could be applied to all Pentecostal churches. He also prophesied about a last day worldwide "layman's revival" which would feature "men and women with ordinary jobs in the ordinary world." In conversations with Demos, Price prophesied that somehow Shakarian would play a part in this last great revival before the rapture of the Church.[3]

The particular prophecy linking Shakarian with this revival was given in 1944 during a conversation between Price and Shakarian. "Demos," said Price:

> "You're about to witness one of the major events foretold in the Bible. 'And it shall come to pass afterward, that I will pour out My Spirit upon all flesh...' It will happen in your lifetime, Demos, and you will play a part in it. This revival will not come through professional preachers ...but will happen spontaneously—all over the world to ordinary men and women—people in shops, offices and factories. I won't live long enough to see it, but you will..."[4]

Even with this stirring prophecy in mind, whenever Shakarian thought of rallying laymen to the cause of revival, he was discouraged by what he saw around him. In most of the revival meetings he attended, he estimated that the women in attendance outnumbered men by a margin of ten to one. He also observed what he described as "a resistance of men to religion," especially among successful businessmen. In a conversation with Price, he stated his impression that "when a man's business starts to succeed, he'll stop coming to church. I've seen it over and over." This was especially true concerning the few successful Pentecostal businessmen that Shakarian had known. Beginning as a religion of the poor and disinherited, the Pentecostal movement had seen many upscale businessmen leave for mainline churches when they began to prosper.[5]

The idea of reaching businessmen was born in Shakarian's mind when he attended the Kiwanis Club to which his father belonged. Seeing the camaraderie and good fellowship, he decided that he would find a service club to which he could belong. After a search of various organizations, he settled on the Lion's Club in his hometown of Downey. While he recognized the value of the services rendered by the club, he confessed to a "longing for a circle of businessmen with a strong spiritual orientation." In 1942, he heard about the Christian Business Men's Committee (CBMC) and promptly organized a chapter in Downey. For two years he served as president of this chapter.

THE HOLLYWOOD BOWL

With the prosperity that came to the nation at the end of World War II, however, a new breed of Pentecostals appeared, successful businessmen with money in the bank who remained faithful to their churches. In time the idea of a businessmen's organization which would harness and preserve this new crop of Pentecostal entrepreneurs became a passionate cause for Shakarian. It was intensified during the euphoric economic boom in America that followed the war.

The meeting that first gave Shakarian national attention was an interdenominational Pentecostal youth rally held in the Los Angeles Shrine Auditorium in 1946. In planning the rally, several Pentecostal leaders asked Shakarian if he would serve as finance chairman and help raise the $300 to rent the auditorium and pay for the advertising. Although at the time, the $300 seemed to be an impossibly large figure, it wasn't nearly enough to do the job: Shakarian challenged them to raise $3,000 instead.

At Shakarian's suggestion, a group of businessmen were invited to a free chicken dinner at Knott's Berry Farm which would be paid for by Demos and his father Isaac. The businessmen were advised only that an offering for the youth rally would be received after the dinner. When the meeting convened, the place was packed. As Demos led the proceedings, the men began to testify about the blessings of the Lord in their lives. For over an hour and a half the testimonies continued until the room seemed to be "flooded with a kind of visible power." Over fried chicken, the businessmen enjoyed good fellowship, fervent prayer. And although the budget for the Hollywood Bowl rally was only $5,500, a surprising offering of $6,200 was received. It was in this dinner meeting that Shakarian saw a model for future meetings of businessmen, away from church sanctuaries in the neutral but attractive atmosphere of a dinner setting.[6]

The subsequent rally was so well advertised and supported by the Pentecostal churches of the area that over 6,000 persons jammed the auditorium with many hundreds outside who couldn't get in. According to Shakarian, a young evangelist named R.W. Culpepper began preaching to those outside, and a "mighty revival" was sparked outside that soon moved inside the building. By all accounts, the rally was a smashing success.[7]

Also, to the delight of Shakarian and the planning committee, the offering was so generous that $5,000 was left over to help pay for another rally in the future. In fact, the glittering success of the Shrine Auditorium meeting emboldened Shakarian and others to lift their sights and dream of filling the most famous outdoor amphitheater in America, the Hollywood Bowl. If the Bowl could be filled, he thought, it would of necessity catch the attention of the world and demonstrate the power of the growing Pentecostal movement. It was indeed an ambitious dream, but as Shakarian's enthusiasm spread, more people joined with him in believing that it very well could happen. By 1948, a groundswell of support encouraged Shakarian to call for a committee to plan a huge rally to fill the 21,000 seats in the Bowl.

The meeting which followed became legendary in California as well as in other areas of the nation. Hundreds of churches participated, bringing thousands of young people to the famous amphitheater of the Hollywood Bowl. The Bowl overflowed with no less than 21,000 persons in attendance, most of them teenagers. The main speaker in the amphitheater was Ray Hughes, a young evangelist from the Church of God, who Shakarian had recruited during a previous trip to Cleveland, Tennessee. The churches which Shakarian brought together represented the Assemblies of God, the International Church of the Foursquare Gospel, the Pentecostal Holiness Church, the Church of God (Cleveland, Tenn.), and the Pentecostal Church of God, as well as dozens of independent Pentecostal congregations, including his own Armenian Pentecostal Church.

Not only were the various Pentecostal churches represented in the Bowl, some of the leading Pentecostal denominational figures were on the platform, including Ernest S. Williams, and Wesley Steelberg (Assemblies of God), Rolf McPherson and Harold Chalfant (Foursquare Gospel), David du Plessis, (a leader of the World Pentecostal Conference), H.L. Chesser and Ray Hughes (Church of God), and Cecil Pool (Pentecostal Church of God). Bringing these leaders together on the same platform was an incredible accomplishment for a layman such as Shakarian.[8]

The service featured a 100-piece symphonic orchestra, and a 360-voice youth choir. Howard Rusthoi, Associate Pastor of Angelus Temple said of the rally: "Never before in history has there been so great a youth rally in all the world." After Hughes' evangelistic message, hundreds of young people filed forward for salvation. The leaders on the platform took note of the large crowd and pondered the implications for the future.

The Hollywood Bowl rally launched both Shakarian and Hughes on the national scene, winning the admiration of Christian leaders around the country. In grudging admiration, Rev. Bob Shuler, a Methodist pastor in Los Angeles, known as an insistent critic of Aimee Semple McPherson said, "the Methodists would not dare try it, but God and the Pentecostals did it." Behind it all, was Demos Shakarian and the businessmen who planned and financed the rally over fried chicken at Knott's Berry Farm.[9]

Soon people around the nation became curious as to who Shakarian was and how he had accomplished such a feat as filling the Hollywood Bowl. His work did not escape the notice of the influential Donald Gee, editor of *Pentecost* magazine which was published in Great Britain. Running an article from *Healing Today* magazine, Gee informed his readers that:

> "This (the Hollywood Bowl rally) put the Pentecostals over the top for God. There is hardly any task too hard for Brother Shakarian. He is a big businessman here, owning one of the largest dairies in the country. His drive-in dairy serves 1500 customers daily, and this is only part of his work. The great story is that he doesn't spend all his time for himself but gives God time, money, and a life of service.[10]

The Hollywood Bowl success continued long after the meeting ended. The money left over was put into a bank account to fund future mass events. In 1956, when the Pentecostals of America celebrated the 50th anniversary of the Azusa Street Revival (1906-1909), the money left over from the Hollywood Bowl rally served as seed money to launch the "Golden Jubilee" celebration which met in the famous Angelus Temple in Los Angeles.[11]

THE BILLY GRAHAM LOS ANGELES CRUSADE

Shakarian also played a behind-the-scenes role in the 1949 Los Angeles tent crusade that launched the ministry of Billy Graham on the national level. Even before William Randolph Hearst had told his newspapers to "puff Graham," Shakarian had directed the Pentecostals at the end of a five-week tent crusade in Anaheim to attend Graham's meeting en masse and "pray for the Holy Ghost to fall" on Graham and his crusade. Before the Pentecostals came in October, Graham had "struggled" for three weeks with few conversions and smaller than expected crowds.

As Graham and his team considered ending the crusade, a sudden upsurge in attendance encouraged him to continue for several more weeks. Many of the new attendees had come at Shakarian's urging. The conversion of Stuart Hamblen and Jim Vaus in November, along with the Hearst support made the Los Angeles crusade the turning point in Graham's ministry. At the height of the eight-week long meeting which ended on November 20 with over 9,000 in attendance under the crusade tent, a large proportion of his hearers (estimated at 25%) were Pentecostals who had followed Shakarian to the Graham tent. For the rest of his life, Shakarian was convinced that without the crucial support of the Pentecostals, the Graham crusade might have been a failure. As it turned out, the 1949 Los Angeles crusade established the young Tar Heel preacher as the major evangelist of his time.[12]

The Graham experience demonstrated an important fact about Shakarian and his Pentecostal friends. It was their willingness to support evangelicals who were not themselves Pentecostals. In future years Graham would acknowledge his debt to the Pentecostals who supported his crusades, not only in Los Angeles, but in all parts of the world. He showed his appreciation by dedicating the newly constructed campus of Oral Roberts University in 1967.[13]

Another way Shakarian expressed his solidarity with other evangelicals was through his membership in the Christian Business Men's Committee (CBMC), a group of laymen from most of the evangelical churches. With meetings similar to the Lions, Kiwanis and Rotary clubs, these men met weekly to share fellowship and testimonies. Shakarian was no stranger to the service club format. While his father was a member of the Downey Kiwanis Club, Demos found his place in the local Lion's Club. In the CBMC, however, the members used the meetings as an avenue of converting businessmen friends to the Lord. Shakarian was not just a casual visitor to the CBMC. In 1942 he served as founder and and for the first two years as president of the Downey, California chapter.

> "Each Saturday morning 30 or 40 of us gathered at Oddfellows Hall to cook our own breakfast, share what God was doing in our lives, discuss the Scriptures, encourage one another, and pray. These men were Methodists, Baptists, Presbyterians, Catholics and Pentecostals, and although we worshiped in different ways, I found that we all loved Jesus. God, indeed, is no

respector of persons, or denominations, and we
could work together well."[14]

As wonderful as the CBMC was at this time, it left
something lacking in Shakarian's mind. These men
"loved Jesus" but there was no spirit or fire in the
meetings. Although "many Spirit-filled men were
members of CBMC" they were "becoming diluted in
their spiritual fervor." Something else needed to be
done. Even the Pentecostal churches were becoming
lukewarm. In some of them, according to Shakarian,
the Holy Spirit was "somewhat boxed in" and even at
that, few businessmen were willing to even enter one
of them.[15]

It was in the CBMC meetings that Shakarian
learned much about how to organize and run a local
chapter of this type of organization. The only problem
with the CBMC chapters, in his mind, was that there
was little of the "Spirit" in the meetings, never a time
when the "glory" could come down. Usually the Pentecostals, out of respect for the ecumenical nature of
the organization, were forced to mute their spirituality
and refrain from praying for the sick or in manifesting
such gifts of the Spirit as prophecy and speaking in
tongues. Although he was a faithful member of the
Downey CBMC chapter, Shakarian channeled most of
his energies into crusades with Pentecostal evangelists.

Each year Shakarian would invite new evangelists
to hold tent meetings in the Los Angeles area. Usually
he served as finance chairman of the crusades, taking
care of all the details of arranging permits, renting and
setting up the tent. His major task, however, was to
raise the budgets to pay for the meetings. Often he paid
much of the costs himself. At one time Rose com-
plained, "every time we saved two or three thousand
dollars in the bank, Demos would smell sawdust, and
we knew it was time for a revival meeting."[16]

By 1950, another major evangelist, Oral Roberts, was appearing on the horizon, a man who would play a crucial role in the founding and development of FGBMFI. Roberts, a young Pentecostal Holiness preacher from Oklahoma had begun a healing ministry in 1948 after serving pastorates in Oklahoma, Georgia, and North Carolina. When Shakarian learned of his ministry, he immediately made plans to invite Roberts to Los Angeles to conduct a major crusade. In the fall of 1951 Roberts came to conduct his first Los Angeles crusade, largely at the invitation of Shakarian and his friends. The ensuing campaign was one of the largest evangelistic crusades in the history of the city with over 200,000 attending the crusade services. As usual, Shakarian served as the finance chairman. After hearing Roberts preach, Shakarian declared that "without reservation, Oral Roberts is today the world's most powerful preacher."[17]

Through all these meetings, Shakarian served in the background as a planner, fund-raiser, and organizer. During this period, he accepted the fact that he was to be a "helper" rather than a star preacher. In fact he explained to his friends:

> "I believe God has a particular gift for each of His servants...I believe that if we find that gift— and use it—we'll be the *happiest people on earth*... I'm lucky, I've found my job. I'm a helper. My gift is to help other people do what they do best. I'll help you get together, help you set up a meeting place, help you find speakers. What I'll get out of it is the joy of using the talent God gave me."[18]

He also found that being a member of a small Armenian Pentecostal congregation turned out to be an asset rather than a liability in his relations with the Pentecostal denominational churches. Perhaps he was not a threat to any church and definitely was not involved in the denominational rivalries that often prevented ecumenical cooperation. As a layman, he could offer help without any question of his having ulterior motives.

These years from 1940 to 1951 were extraordinary times for Shakarian as well as for Pentecostalism at large. Even before the organization of FGBMFI, Shakarian had already made a mark in evangelism. From his first meetings in Lincoln Park in 1940 to the Roberts crusade in 1951, the crusades, tent meetings, and rallies organized by Shakarian had already attracted more than 1,000,000 persons, and thousands of them had been converted including many businessmen.[19]

But the best was yet to come.

1. *For vivid descriptions of the Lincoln Park meetings see Sherrill,* Happiest People on Earth, *pp. 54-58.*

2. Ibid., *pp. 61-64.*

3. *Sherrill,* Happiest People on Earth, *pp. 80-83; Durasoff,* Bright Wind, *pp. 145; Also see* Ibid., *January, 1954, pp. 11-13.*

4. *Sherrill,* Ibid., *pp. 87-97. Charles R. Conn, "Ray Hughes," in Burgess,* et. al., Dictionary of Pentecostal and Charismatic Movements, *p. 451.*

5. *Shakarian-Synan interview, October, 5, 1987, pp. 10-11.*

6. *Sherrill,* Happiest People on Earth, *pp. 87-89.*

7. *The most detailed account of the Shrine Auditorium rally is given in* The Amazing Shakarian Story, *pp. 29-30.*

8. *For an effusive description of the Bowl rally see: Harold C. Herman, "Christ Came to Hollywood Bowl,"* The Pentecostal Evangel, *October 23, 1948, p.13.*

9. *Sherrill,* Ibid., *pp. 87-97. Charles R. Conn, "Ray Hughes," in Burgess,* et. al., Dictionary of Pentecostal and Charismatic Movements, *p. 451. Demos Shakarian, "The Shakarian Story,"* Healing Waters Magazine, *March, 1953, pp. 6-11. For reflections on the importance of the Hollywood Bowl rally among Pentecostals see: John Nichol,* Pentecostalism *(New York: Harper & Row, 1966), p. 217; Herman,* Christ Came to Hollywood Bowl, *p. 13.*

10. *Luther Carroll, Jr. "The Man Behind That Memorable Hollywood Bowl Meeting,"* Pentecost, *June, 1953, p. 18.*

11. *See "The True Azusa Story,"* Voice, *September, 1956, pp.3-17; and "The Golden Jubilee Will Continue in Our Hearts," October, 1956, pp. 3-5.*

12. *Shakarian-Synan interview, October, 6, 1987, pp.10-11. Shakarian estimated that at least 20% of Graham's hearers in Los Angeles were Pentecostals from the Anaheim crusade. For information on the Graham crusade, see John Pollock's* Bill Graham; The Authorized Biography *(New York: McGraw Hill, 1966), pp. 53-64. It seems that Graham used a "word of knowledge" to identify Stuart Hamblen as a "man who was living a double life." Hamblen's subsequent conversion added to the fame of the Los Angeles crusade.*

13. *David Edwin Harrell,* Oral Roberts; An American Life *(Bloomington: Indiana University Press, 1985), pp. 228-230.*

14. *Demos Shakarian, "A Prophecy Fulfilled,"* Voice, *July 1982, p. 18.*

15. Ibid., *pp. 19-20.*

16. *Synan-Shakarian interview, p. 17.*

17. *See Harrell,* Oral Roberts; An American Life, *p. 97. Also see Harrell's* All Things Are Possible *(Bloomington: Indiana University Press, 1975), pp.41-52, 151-159, 146-47.*

18. *This philosophy is given in Sherrill's* Happiest People on Earth, *p. 101.*

19. *Synan-Shakarian interview, February 2, 1988, p. 17.*

Chapter Four

THE BIRTH OF
THE FELLOWSHIP

*If I remember, there were 21 present that morning
when we had breakfast...and Demos presented me
and I spoke...I said, "Why don't we sing 'Onward
Christian Soldiers'?"*
And we did, and the Holy Ghost fell.—Oral Roberts

The success of the Hollywood Bowl rally in 1948
ignited a fire in Shakarian's soul to start a laymen's organization that could do for the nation what he had seen
done in the Hollywood Bowl. He never forgot the dinner meeting of businessmen at Knott's Berry Farm and
the fervent testimonies that came from the dedicated
Spirit-filled laymen. It seemed that they had been voice-
less in the past, but if the anointing and power upon
laymen that produced the Hollywood Bowl rally and
the Oral Roberts Los Angeles crusade could be harnessed
and directed, it would truly become a force in the earth.
Perhaps an army of Spirit-filled businessmen could be
the vanguard of the great "laymen's revival" that
Charles Price had predicted many years before.

It was Oral Roberts, the rising star among evangelists, who served as a catalyst for bringing Shakarian's
dream of a Spirit-filled laymen's organization into being.
In 1951, Demos and his father, Isaac, joined with others

in inviting Roberts to bring his "tent cathedral" to Los
Angeles. Since Isaac served on the State Board of Agri-
culture, he was able to obtain the permits for Oral to set
up his tent on the Fairgrounds. Demos, as usual, served
as finance chairman. He also served as general local
chairman for planning the entire crusade. At night
Demos' son Richard served as Roberts' chauffeur to
and from the crusade meetings. It was during this meeting that Shakarian shared with the tall Oklahoma healing evangelist his vision of a "Full Gospel" organization
for businessmen. Over coffee in an all-night diner in the
Ambassador Hotel, he poured out his vision to Roberts,
who listened intently as he explained his concept of a:

> "group of men. Not exceptional men. Just
> average business people who know the Lord and
> love Him, but haven't known how to show it."
> These would be men who "tell other men...like
> themselves...who might not believe what a
> preacher said—even someone like you—but
> who will listen to a plumber or a dentist or a
> salesman because they're plumbers and dentists
> and salesmen themselves."[1]

He even had a name for the new group, "Full
Gospel Business Men's Fellowship International," a
name that Roberts called "quite a mouthful." Empha-
sizing the importance of each word, Shakarian
explained the nature of the organization as follows:

> *"Full Gospel"* This meant that no subject would
> have to be avoided at our meetings. Healing.
> Tongues. Deliverance. Whatever the man's ex-
> perience, he could talk about it, just as it
> happened.
> *"Business Men"* Laymen. Ordinary people.
> *"Fellowship"* That's what it should feel like. A
> bunch of people who love to get together—not
> rules and committees and meeting-come-to-
> order kind of thing.

"International" ...The whole world. All flesh.[2]

Upon hearing this vision, Roberts said, "something clicked in my heart" prompting him to immediately offer his support. "Why don't you start?" he asked Shakarian, "Why don't you gather as many men together as you can Saturday morning at Clifton's Cafeteria (where he told me they had a breakfast now and then) ...and I will speak for you and share the vision with them as you have shared it with me." In addition, Roberts suggested that Shakarian recruit Lee Braxton to help found the new Fellowship. "He is my right-hand man from the business world, a dollar-a-year man, one of the most successful men in America." At Roberts' suggestion, Bob Deweese presented Shakarian and Braxton to an overflow crowd of 12,500 people at the crusade. Before this huge crowd, they invited businessmen to the breakfast meeting the next morning in the cafeteria. Roberts also warmly endorsed the invitation. In agreement, Shakarian invited Roberts to be the main speaker for the event.[3]

CLIFTON'S CAFETERIA

The meeting took place in Clifton's Cafeteria in downtown Los Angeles on Broadway and Seventh on Saturday morning, October 13, 1951. Since the breakfast had been announced from the Roberts' crusade platform before thousands of people, Shakarian was sure that hundreds of laymen would come to hear the famous preacher. When Saturday morning arrived for the breakfast meeting, however, he was profoundly disappointed when only 21 businessmen showed up. But, of great importance for the future, Lee Braxton, the first vice-president of FGBMFI was present.[4]

Despite the "lack of enthusiasm" in the room, the meeting went forward with Rose playing the organ and leading in a few songs. Then Demos made a short speech explaining the purpose of the new fellowship:

> "God's Spirit in the next decade will seek new channels to move in...No organs. No stained glass. Nothing that men can pigeonhole as 'religious'. Just one man telling another about Jesus."[5]

All around the room, he saw some men looking at their watches. He knew that they were busy men, "the kind who won't waste a minute on an outfit that isn't going anywhere." He was seized with a fear that the meeting might end in total failure.

Any disappointment on Shakarian's part didn't seem to effect Roberts. Ignoring the sparse crowd, the evangelist enthusiastically endorsed Shakarian's vision for the new organization and challenged the businessmen to forge ahead. In his closing prayer Roberts electrified the group with a prophetic prayer:

> "Lord Jesus," he prayed, "let this fellowship grow in Your strength alone. Send it marching in Your power across the nation. Across the world. We give You thanks right now, Lord Jesus, that we see a little group of people in a cafeteria, but You see a thousand chapters."[6]

Suddenly, the mood in the room changed. The challenge of starting 1000 chapters "electrified the room." In closing the meeting, Oral led the group in singing "Onward Christian Soldiers." In true Pentecostal style, they formed a "Jericho march" and went around the room shouting praises to God. As Roberts later said, "the Holy Ghost fell." The small group that gathered that morning in Clifton's Cafeteria later became the first chapter of Full Gospel Business Men's Fellowship International.[7]

After this first breakfast, a decision was made to meet each week at Clifton's, but the momentum of

Roberts' challenge was less than overwhelming. From week to week the attendance varied between 15 and 40 men. Although the crowds were small, some people of future importance were regular attendants. Among these were John McTernan, a future missionary to Italy, and Ray Bringham, an early "neo-pentecostal" from the Church of God, Anderson, Indiana. Most of the time Shakarian paid for the entire cost of the meals. Despite the testimonies, music, and ministry, there was a notable lack of enthusiasm in most of the meetings. In order to spark interest, Shakarian wrote letters, made phone calls, invited old friends, and asked local Pentecostal pastors to make announcements from their pulpits. All this activity, however, seemed to make little difference. The crowds remained small.[8]

In spite of these problems in Los Angeles, Shakarian moved rapidly to promote the new fellowship in other parts of the nation. The success of the Roberts' crusade led him to fly to the next one which was held in November of 1951 in Fresno, California. Again Roberts offered Shakarian full support from the platform. As in Los Angeles, on the final Saturday morning of the crusade, a meeting of businessmen was called in a local restaurant on November 17. Roberts again addressed the gathering, which this time numbered 150 men. In his address, Roberts advised the men to hold a business meeting and form a temporary organization which could be given legal status later. He also advised them to adopt the name "Full Gospel Business Men" rather than "Pentecostal" or "Christian" so they would be clearly identified and "people would not be fooled." He further advised them not to allow preachers to be members lest they take it over and change its purpose. "You should use us…and ask us for advice," but in the end "it is your vision" he said.[9]

After Roberts' message, the group immediately

held its first official business meeting. The first decision was to name the new group "Full Gospel Business Men's Fellowship of America." The second action was to elect a slate of pro tem officers. Those elected were; President, Demos Shakarian (Downey, California, dairyman and real estate developer), Vice-Presidents, Lee Braxton (Whiteville, North Carolina, banker and automotive dealer and president of 21 corporations), George Gardner (Binghampton, New York, immediate past president of the New York State Automobile Dealers Association), Miner Arganbright (La Crescenta, California, masonry and building contractor), and Secretary-Treasurer, Earl Draper (Fresno, California, realtor and accountant). These officers gave the organization "nationwide representation" and indicated by the words "of America" in its name that the vision at this point was primarily for the United States. The worldwide organization could come in due time.[10]

In January of 1952, Shakarian flew to Phoenix to attend the Roberts' crusade and promote the new fellowship among the masses of people that flocked to his tent crusade there. Again a breakfast meeting was announced from the platform. At this meeting over 100 men attended the gathering which was led by Shakarian. Again Roberts spoke to the businessmen and highly recommended that they join Shakarian in his efforts. The major action of the Phoenix meeting was to retain an attorney, Paul B. Fischer of Santa Ana, California to draw up a proposed articles of incorporation.[11]

Even with these successes on the national level, things continued to progress at a snail's pace in the Los Angeles chapter. At times it seemed that what Shakarian received for his efforts in Los Angeles was mostly criticism. Some local pastors saw FGMBFI as a possible new denomination, or as competition for tithes and offerings. "Churches eyed the new fellowship with suspicion," Shakarian lamented. During the entire year, he reported, the Fellowship received not one single donation. In a desperate effort to drum up support, Demos bought time on a local radio station and began a half-hour "breakfast broadcast" each Saturday which originated partly from the cafeteria meetings. He also traveled widely across the United States trying to work up enthusiasm for the new group, but little good seemed to come from all this effort. By June, he was dispirited and exhausted.[12]

The next few months were extremely discouraging for Shakarian and almost fatal for his dream of a laymen's fellowship. Many of those attending the meeting in Clifton's Cafeteria offered free advice and criticism about how things were being run. At one point his wife, Rose, advised him to give up on the whole idea, but Shakarian forged straight ahead despite the criticism. Despite his determination, he was painfully aware that even though large numbers of men had gathered in the Fresno and Phoenix meetings during the Oral Roberts crusades, no second chapter was formed during the year.[13]

Another disappointment came in 1952 after Shakarian met with David du Plessis, a Pentecostal leader who had helped inaugurate the first Pentecostal World Conference in Zurich in 1947. After speaking in a meeting in Clifton's Cafeteria, du Plessis suggested that Shakarian go with him to London for the Pentecostal World Conference and offer his idea of a new businessmen's fellowship to the pentecostal churches of the world. After traveling to London on his first overseas commercial flight, Shakarian and du Plessis offered the idea of their organization to the leaders of the presidium. The response was immediate and unexpectedly negative. They were summarily turned down by the fathers of world pentecostalism. Not a single leader voted to accept the offer of a worldwide Full Gospel Business Men's Fellowship.[14]

Despite this rebuff, when he returned to the United States, Shakarian moved forward with his plans to create a legal basis for the new organization. For several months he and Fischer labored over a draft of a new constitution which could serve as the basis of an application for a charter in the state of California. When they were satisfied with the document, they called for a meeting of the *pro tem* officers that had been selected in Fresno. All of them were able to come to the meeting except Lee Braxton. In the meantime, a printer from Watsonville, California, Thomas R. Nickel, had offered his print shop and editorial services to produce a magazine for the new organization. Although he received no response in Fresno in November, he was invited to the incorporation meeting which met in the "Clifton's Upper Room" in Los Angeles.[15]

A major change in the name and purpose of the Fellowship was evident in the name that was chosen for the charter. In Fresno it had been called "Full Gospel Business Men of *America*." Now it would henceforth be known as the "Full Gospel Business Men's Fellowship *International*." In other words, the vision had been enlarged to include not only America, but the entire world.[16]

After adopting the new "Constitution and Bylaws" and the "Articles of Incorporation," these documents were signed by the officers present. The first action taken by the new body was the selection of Nickel as editor of the new official organ of the group which was named *Full Gospel Voice*. Then a special message was delivered to the historic gathering by G.H. Montgomery, editor of Oral Roberts' *Healing Waters Magazine*.[17]

Even with all this activity on an organizational level, the Los Angeles chapter seemed to show few signs of life. Attendance continued to be uneven. The low point for Shakarian came in December 1952 when Miner Arganbright, an old business friend, told him, "You don't know when you're whipped. I wouldn't give five cents for this outfit."[18] This advice from Arganbright seemed to stab Shakarian in the heart. During the following week, he made up his mind to abandon the whole idea of a men's fellowship entirely. By Friday night, he had decided that the next meeting in Clifton's Cafeteria would be his last.

THE VISION

Just as he was about to give up in despair, Shakarian experienced a transforming vision which infused him with an inspiration and zeal that re-ignited his dreams. On Friday night December 26, 1952 the Shakarians had in their home a houseguest, Tommy Hicks, a little-known Pentecostal evangelist. That night, Shakarian confided to Hicks that since so little interest had been shown in his idea, the next day would be the last meeting in Clifton's Cafeteria. Late that evening, Shakarian suggested that everyone else in the house go to bed while he went into the living room to pray "till he heard from God, no matter how long it took." His place of prayer was the red Oriental rug that covered the living room floor. As he began to pray it seemed that "the heavens were made of brass." Then he experienced a vision that forever changed his life and that of the infant FGBMFI organization. As the vision continued, his wife, Rose, came into the room and began playing the organ softly. The experience that followed not only changed the course of his life, but the future course of Full Gospel Business Men's Fellowship.[19]

In an apparent ecstasy lasting for several hours, Shakarian was taken around the world in a vision where he was able to see all the continents from the air. As he looked down, he could see, as through a tele-photo lens, men as frozen statues, cold and lifeless. In Africa, Latin America, Europe, and Asia, he saw the same scene, "brown faces, black faces, white faces—everyone rigid, wretched, each locked in its own private death." Then he made another circuit of the globe and this time millions of people had come to life. "This time heads were raised, eyes shone with joy. Hands were lifted towards heaven...everywhere death had turned to life." At this point, Rose, while playing the organ, began to prophesy words of encouragement saying: "You are in the will of the Lord and it was for this reason that you were born." Then she spoke in tongues and again prophesied saying, "That which you see now will soon come to pass." Meanwhile, Tommy Hicks, who was in the guest bedroom, was receiving a similar vision for a great revival in Argentina.[20]

The next morning at Clifton's the entire spirit of the meeting had changed. Arganbright, who earlier would not give five cents for the future of the organiza-tion, gave Shakarian a check for $1000 saying that he had been awakened in the middle of the night with in-structions from the Lord to give the money. Also com-ing forward was Thomas R. Nickel, the printer from Watsonville, California who was unable to sleep the night before. As Shakarian was having his vision, Nickel felt compelled to get in his automobile and drive the 400 miles to Los Angeles. After driving most of the night, he arrived at Clifton's just as the meeting started. After Arganbright gave his check for $1000, Nickel came forward and urged the immediate publication of the first edition of *Voice* magazine. Both Arganbright and Nickel repeated phrases that Shakarian heard in the vision a few hours before: "This organization must go around the world." Overnight, the dream of a world-wide businessmen's fellowship had been resurrected, not only in Shakarian's mind, but in the minds of others who could render the services needed to make it a success.[21]

FGBMFI

In the full flush of inspiration, Shakarian moved quickly to have the "Constitution and Bylaws" official-ly incorporated by the State of California. The charter, which now used the name "Full Gospel Business Men's Fellowship International," was officially recognized by the State of California on January 2, 1953 as a non-profit religious organization. The *Constitution and By-Laws* required that all members subscribe to the "Doctrinal Statement" which was described not as a creed, but as "minimal biblical doctrinal tests...the re-jection of any of which shall be grounds for ineligibility to membership." The FGBMFI document was based on the "Articles of Faith" of the Pentecostal Fellowship of North America (PFNA).[22]

Thus, the FGBMFI statement required members to believe in the Trinity (thus excluding the "Oneness" Pentecostals), that the Bible was "infallible" (the word "inerrant" was not used), in "sanctification by the blood of Christ" (thus including the holiness wing of the Pentecostal movement), in "divine healing, through faith...and that healing is in the atonement" (thus opening the way for the Fellowship to play a lead-ing role in the rising tide of the faith healing move-ment), and "in the baptism in the Holy Ghost accom-panied by the initial physical sign of speaking in other tongues as the Spirit gives utterance" (making the or-

ganization fully "pentecostal" in doctrine and
practice).[23]

In order to preserve the lay character of the organization, the clergy, defined as "Pastors, Evangelists,
Missionaries, and other full-time Gospel Workers"
were invited to be members but were not allowed to
"hold leading official positions, or direct the activities
of the organization." Although women were made welcome at the meetings it was understood that the name
made the fellowship a laymen's group. Full membership would be open only to males. The definition of
eligibility for membership stated that "the term Business Men's or Business Man has a liberal meaning including primarily all men of any secular occupation as
well as farmers, laborers, and employees." Envisioning
future growth outside the United States, the word "International" was used and emphasized.[24]

The first issue of *Voice* featured articles by or
about the founding fathers, i.e. Shakarian the dairyman, Arganbright the masonry contractor, Gardner the
automobile dealer, and Lee Braxton the banker, who at
the time also served as the director of Oral Roberts'
radio and television ministries. These lay testimonies
became a standard feature in all future issues of *Voice.*
The only clergyman featured in this first issue was G.H.
Montgomery, editor of Oral Roberts' *Healing Waters*
magazine, whose article was a written version of the
message he had delivered at the signing of the "Articles
of Incorporation."[25]

On February 7, 1953, a day that Shakarian described as "momentous," the Los Angeles Chapter conducted a dedication service for the new magazine.
Nickel was asked to fly from Watsonville with 1000
copies of the first edition of the freshly-printed magazines. The masthead had been designed by Tommy
Hicks. The golden text on page 2 was from Proverbs

8:4 "Unto You, O men, I call: and my voice is to the sons of men."

After the dedication, all the men were invited to attend a "Full Gospel Holy Ghost Rally" at a local Assemblies of God Church in Bell Gardens, California. The announcement of *Voice* was warmly received at the rally when Shakarian explained that this new publication would "go into all the world and preach the Gospel to every creature." [26]

It was a happy group of men who left the rally in Bell Gardens that night. They now possessed not only an organization with gifted leaders, but they also had a "voice" that would indeed help FGBMFI "go into all the world." They also carried with them a world vision that would eventually carry the work of the Fellowship to most of the nations of the world. In their leader, Demos Shakarian they had a young man with unbounded vitality, vision, and faith. Indeed, when he and Oral Roberts conducted the first chapter meeting in 1951, Oral was only 34 years old while Shakarian was only in his 38th year.

For all the years after the organization of FGMBFI, Shakarian was convinced that without his vision of millions of men around the world coming from stony death to vibrant life the Fellowship would have died an early and inglorious death. The vision, in fact, turned out to be the great turning point in the early history of the Fellowship.

1. *Sherrill,* Happiest People on Earth, *pp. 117-118. Oral Roberts, personal interview with the author, October 10, 1991, Tulsa, Oklahoma, p. 1.*

2. Ibid., *pp. 118-119.*

3. *Oral Roberts, personal interview with the author, October 10, 1991, (Tulsa, Oklahoma), p. 1.*

4. *Ibid.,* p. 119.

5. Sherrill, Happiest People on Earth, *p.120.*

6. Ibid., *p. 120.*

7. *Shakarian "How Our Fellowship Came into Being," pp. 3-5. Also see Sherrill,* Happiest People on Earth, *pp.117-121; Shakarian-Synan Interview, October 5, 1987, pp. 13-15; and Brian Bird, "The Legacy of Demos Shakarian,"* Charisma, *June, 1986, pp. 21-25. For the role or Oral Roberts see Harrell,* Oral Roberts; An American Life, *pp. 97, 153-155.*

8. *Sherrill,* Happiest People on Earth, pp. 121-122.

9. Roberts-Synan interview, pp.6-7.

10. See "Full Gospel Business Men of America Start New National Association" Healing Waters Magazine, *January, 1952, p. 12. This periodical was the national publication of the Oral Roberts ministry.*

11. *See Shakarian, "How Our Fellowship Came into Being" pp. 3-5.*

12. *Sherrill,* Happiest People on Earth, *pp. 121-122.*

13. *Sherrill,* Ibid., *pp. 129-130; Shakarian-Synan Interview, October 5, 1987, pp. 14-15.*

14. *The account of the London trip with David du Plessis is given in Sherrill,* Ibid., *122-124. It was not mentioned in any other of Shakarian's accounts.*

15. *See "Full Gospel Business Men"* Healing Waters, *January, 1953, p.. 13; and Shakarian, "How our Fellowship Came into Being," pp. 4-5.*

16. *See* The Constitution and By-laws and Articles of Incorporation of Full Gospel Business Men's Fellowship International *(Costa Mesa, California: 1985), pp. 3-8.*

17. *See G. H. Montgomery, "God's Contract With Us"* Voice, *February, 1953, pp. 2-15.*

18. *Sherrill,* Ibid., *pp. 129-130; Shakarian-Synan interview, October 5, 1987, pp 14-15.*

19. Ibid., *pp. 130-134. The rug is enshrined at the FGBMFI Headquarters in Costa Mesa, California.*

20. *Sherrill,* Happiest People on Earth, *pp. 133-134. This vision was told and retold in most of Shakarian's accounts of the history of FGBMFI with several variations. In his first account in* Voice *(February, 1953) he gave the date of the vision as being on "May 2, 1952." In some accounts Shakarian indicates that Nickel made his initial offer of printing a magazine on December 30, 1952, the morning after the Shakarian vision. But this scenario does not stand if Nickel was officially commissioned to publish the magazine on November 22, 1952, a month before the vision. Since the Arganbright*

check shows a date of December 30, 1952, the December date seems to be correct. Therefore, Nickel's offer on December 27, must have been to move immediately on the Voice *project which had already been authorized.*

21. *Sherrill*, Ibid., *pp. 135-136.*

22. *See* Voice, *February, 1953, p. 16; October, 1953, pp.5-7.*

23. Articles of Incorporation and By-laws of the Full Gospel Business Men's Fellowship International *(Revised to 1977), pp. 1-6. The "Doctrinal Statement" was published on the back cover of* Voice *from January of 1954 through January of 1955. Also see* Voice, *March 1953 for the "Preamble" March 1953, p. 7. The prominent ministry of the "Oneness" evangelist William Branham was a glaring exception to the doctrinal norms of the Fellowship.*

24. *See* Articles of Incorporation, *1977, p. 8; and* Constitution and By-laws Revised to 1986.

25. *Demos Shakarian, "Official Dedication of Full Gospel Men's* Voice," Voice, *March, 1953, p.3.*

26. Ibid.

Chapter Five

A NATIONWIDE MOVEMENT

"Businessmen need the fellowship of other businessmen. They speak each other's language."
—Lee Braxton

The official organization of the Fellowship and the publication of *Voice* magazine opened the way for rapid growth and the organization of new chapters in America. If FGBMFI was indeed destined to spread throughout the world, first it was necessary to build a strong base in the United States, the country of its birth. And growth in America was not long in coming, thanks largely to the zealous work of Tommy Hicks.

For over a year the Fellowship had consisted of only one chapter, the original one in Los Angeles, which continued to meet weekly on Saturdays in Clifton's Cafeteria. During 1953, soon after the Fellowship was recognized by the State of California, attendance at Clifton's mushroomed. From the 15 to 40 men who came for most of 1952, the numbers now often reached 300 to 400. The new *Voice* magazine soon proved to be an invaluable tool for recruiting new members. Also helping to promote the chapter was the weekly "Breakfast-Broadcast" which went out each Saturday over radio station KRKD from 8:30 to 9:00 a.m. As attendance soared, extra chairs were often brought in to handle the overflow crowds.[1]

The organization of the second chapter came early in 1953 at the end of a Tommy Hicks crusade in Sioux Falls, South Dakota. At the close of the last service, Hicks had asked any men who were interested in forming a local FGBMFI chapter to "come down to the front." To his surprise, "it looked like the whole room came forward." An excited Hicks phoned Shakarian and gushed, "You've got yourself Group Number Two here in South Dakota."[2]

In short order, the Sioux Falls chapter was chartered as were new chapters in Washington, D.C.; Pittsburgh, Pennsylvania; Tacoma, Washington; as well as Oakland, Lancaster and Hayward, California. Indicative of things to come was the fact that the Sioux Falls and Washington, D.C. chapters were organized by evangelist Tommy Hicks after closing "miracle" crusades.[3]

As in the case of Sioux Falls and Washington, D.C., most of the new chapters were organized in the wake of crusades conducted by the three leading healing evangelists of the day, Tommy Hicks, Oral Roberts, and William Branham. In a sense, FGBMFI was one of the most important and lasting institutions fostered by the healing movement of the 1950's. Not only did the Fellowship open up new opportunities for the healing evangelists, but, according to David Harrell, it became at one and the same time the "product" and "platform" for the healing revival.[4]

The popularity of the healing evangelists and their support of FGBMFI led to ever more explosive growth for the Fellowship. Soon the volume of mail generated by *Voice* and the opening of new chapters created an urgent need for offices to service the organization. From the beginning, the work of the Fellowship had been handled by Shakarian from his home and from the offices of his Reliance dairy.

A spurt of growth in the summer of 1953 caused an excited Shakarian to write in the July-August edition of *Voice* the following report:

> "Our organization is growing faster than we had anticipated. Members are affiliating, chapters are being organized and subscriptions to Full Gospel Business Men's *Voice* are coming in from all parts of America as well as from foreign countries."[5]

All this activity required workers to handle the increasing workload that Shakarian had previously handled in his home and his offices. By the summer of 1953, when the number of chapters had reached nine, a full-time employee, Floyd Highfield, was hired to answer inquiries and coordinate the organization of new chapters. To house these activities and make room for secretarial help, a building in downtown Los Angeles was secured for the first offices of the Fellowship. The offices were located at 1059 South Hope Street. After a great deal of renovation, the offices were dedicated on July 11, 1953 with Raymond T. Richey of Houston, Texas as the featured speaker. Others present for the ceremony included Tommy Hicks, R.L. Culpepper, David du Plessis, and Miner Arganbright.[6]

As the Fellowship grew, Shakarian took great pains to explain that FGBMFI was not a church but a group of loyal laymen who desired only to contribute to the local churches. Nevertheless, the major Pentecostal denominations were unsure about the future course of the Fellowship and were concerned over the ultimate threat of a possible new denomination issuing from the dynamically growing group. To allay these fears, attorney Paul Fischer explained in *Voice* that "FGBMFI is not a substitute for, or in competition with, the church." He promised furthermore "to cooperate

heartily with all believing churches and pastors." He
further stated that FGBMFI was not a substitute for the
"denominations, (or) other men's fellowships such as
the Gideons or Christian Business Men's Committee."
In fact, Shakarian earlier had founded the Downey,
California chapter of the Christian Business Men's
Committee. Despite these assurances, some Pentecostal
church leaders feared that the Fellowship was in reality
"a subtle rebellion against denominational authority."[7]
Generally, however, most leaders such as Ralph Riggs,
General Superintendent of the Assemblies of God,
adopted a "wait and see" policy regarding future relations with the Fellowship.[8]

Some observers from mainline churches were of-
fended by the very use of the term "Full Gospel."
Voice answered a critic who wrote, "I resent the fact
that you folks use the term Full Gospel. It would indicate that my own denomination does not have the Full
Gospel." The editor replied that the writer's denomination did indeed have the Full Gospel "but did not
believe it, teach it, preach it, or practice it." In another,
less dogmatic article, Lee Braxton admonished his
readers, "It is time to get over denominational barriers.
The Body of Christ is being brought together. The
Scriptures are being fulfilled by our healing
evangelists."[9]

Indeed, the typical chapter meeting was anything
but an ecclesiastical service as experienced by most
Pentecostal churches, much less the mainline churches.
For the most part, FGBMFI chapters met in hotels and
restaurants following the pattern set by the first chapter
in Clifton's Cafeteria. Typical meetings consisted of an
evening banquet preceded by choruses, prayers, and
announcements, followed by testimonies, prayers for
the sick, and calls for salvation to any unbelievers who
might be present. Not uncommon were prophecies and

messages in other tongues followed by interpretations. In time Shakarian found that the manifestations of the charismata helped rather than hindered attendance at the chapters. Also, more than not, banners over the head table proclaimed the unofficial motto of the Fellowship, "His Banner Over Us Is Love," words taken from a popular spiritual chorus based on the Song of Solomon 2:4.[10]

The worship, praise and ministry of these meetings drew businessmen to the new chapters like a magnet. The love and fellowship that overflowed the meetings was different from the usual meetings of service clubs such as the Lions, Rotary, or Kiwanis. The sight of "men hugging men" took some getting used to, especially for first time attenders with no previous exposure to Pentecostalism. One visitor, Thomas Packard, a beauty products salesman from Toledo, Ohio, had learned from his job that "you don't hug another man." But he soon learned about the "agape" love that permeated FGBMFI meetings. He was later converted and baptized in the Holy Spirit.[11]

By the time the new offices were opened, work had begun on planning the first national convention which was announced for October 10-13 in Los Angeles. With little money and much faith, the officers went forward with plans for the convention by reserving hotel and meeting room facilities and inviting speakers.

In the meantime, *Voice* magazine announced the first "name" convert to the cause, Dr. Jerome Stowell, an "atheist scientist" turned into a "Full Gospel Witness for Jesus Christ and the Word of God." Not only was Stowell converted, he also spoke in tongues. His testimony in *Voice*, "A Scientist Discovers God," became the first of hundreds of conversion accounts that would appear over the years.[12]

The first national convention of FGBMFI met in the Clark Hotel in downtown Los Angeles in October of 1953. Here for the first time, members from the nine chapters could meet together, enjoy fellowship and compare notes. The national conventions were large-scale replicas of the local chapter meetings with the added attraction of featuring nationally-known speakers. The number who gathered for this first convention was only 600, but at the time, that seemed like a very large number indeed.

Like later conventions, this one featured an opening breakfast and a closing banquet as well as a mass healing service. Meals were served in the hotel while the mass services were held in the Shrine Auditorium. Featured speakers included such healing luminaries as Jack Coe, Oral Roberts, Raymond T. Richey, Gordon Lindsay, and Tommy Hicks. It was no accident that the convention was timed to coincide with the end of another Oral Roberts crusade in the city. At the close of the meeting, Shakarian stated that "the convention was the most glorious demonstration of the power of God I have ever seen anywhere in my life."[13]

The financial needs of the new organization were met in the same charismatic fashion as all other parts of the program. Although Shakarian and all the officers of FGBMFI worked without salaries, there were expenses that would need to be funded if the organization was to continue its growth. The one full-time employee, Floyd Highfield, would soon need a secretary. There were the office expenses to pay. Also, even though *Voice* was printed at cost in Nickel's print shop in Watsonville, the costs of postage and handling still had to be paid. Shakarian told the 600 delegates and guests that a grand total of $10,000 would be needed to fund all the activities of FGBMFI for the coming year.[14]

The offering for the annual budget was presented

by evangelist Jack Coe, "a huge man with a knack for coming to the point." Standing before the 600 people assembled he said, "We need $10,000...I would like one hundred men to come forward and pledge one hundred dollars each." Immediately a line of men formed before the platform and each one signed a pledge for $100. When the cards were counted, there were exactly 100 men who pledged. "The budget had been raised to the penny," exclaimed an exultant Shakarian.[15]

The success of the first national convention added to the momentum that was now gaining force almost daily. Through the end of 1953 until the convening of the second national convention in October 1954, no less than nine more chapters were formed in the U.S. including chapters in Reading, PA, Springfield and Chicago, IL, Fresno, CA, Pittsburgh, PA, St. Petersburg and Miami, FL, Dallas, TX, and Denver, CO.[16]

In the meantime Tommy Hicks reported back to the headquarters in Los Angeles that a mighty revival had broken out in Argentina. He had met with President Peron and was given free access to the largest stadium in Buenos Aires. By the end of the campaign, Hicks was preaching to over 200,000 in one service in the Hurican Football (Soccer) stadium, where miracles were the order of the day. This crusade proved to be the largest attended evangelistic crusade in the history of Christianity up to that time, impressing people as diverse as the evangelicals and the liberal editors of the *Christian Century*. No less than 300,000 "decision cards" were printed for the crusade. Gordon Lindsay reported to his readers in *The Voice of Healing* that one crowd reached the incredible total of 400,000 people. As reports of the Hicks crusades continued to come in during the spring and summer of 1954, FGBMFI's *Voice* served as the major periodical reporting these historic meetings.[17]

It was in the full flush of excitement over the Argentina crusade that the second convention met in the Shoreham Hotel in Washington, D.C. in June of 1954. Also adding to the excitement was the fact that the number of chapters had doubled during the previous twelve months. Meals were served in the Shoreham while evening sessions were held in Washington's Constitution Hall. The program featured not only Hicks with his reports of the Argentinian victory, but also such other major healing evangelists as Oral Roberts, William Branham, A.C. Valdez, and Jack Coe. In reporting the evening services, Shakarian said:

> "Each night in Constitution Hall marvelous messages were delivered...and many miracles of healing were witnessed. Valdez gripped the great audience with his sincerity and eloquence; Coe's reckless faith amazed many and was rewarded by dramatic healings; Branham's gifts of discernment and healing were manifested to an almost incredible, but nevertheless thrilling, degree."[18]

A striking speaker one day was no less a personage than Richard Nixon, the Vice-President of the United States. According to Shakarian, Nixon's message on "The Minds and Hearts and Souls of Men" stirred everyone present. In future years the Fellowship would feature such politicians as Ronald Reagan and Chicago mayor Richard Daley.[19] At the end of the convention, Shakarian said "This was the greatest convention ever known in the history of Pentecost." No less a person than David du Plessis wrote that the convention had "changed the course" of his life and ministry, causing him to become "more fully" an evangelist. He was especially impressed with the "complete abandonment to the Holy Ghost of those wealthy Full Gospel Business Men." This, he said "was a treat I did not expect.''[20]

The successful conclusion of the 1954 convention indicated that FGBMFI had indeed become a powerful force in American Christianity. A major factor in this early growth was the barnstorming travel of Demos Shakarian around the country promoting the Fellowship. Often he flew with his friend, C.C. Ford, a real estate developer from Denver, Colorado, who piloted his own plane. At other times he flew with his Vice-President, Lee Braxton who also flew his own craft. The tireless travels of the President and his officers contributed in a major way to the ongoing growth of the Fellowship.[21]

The abandonment to the Holy Spirit that so impressed du Plessis in 1954 was nowhere more apparent than in the youth sessions that were conducted in conjunction with the world conventions. Some of the early youth organizers were Jack Shaw of South Carolina, Jamie Brown of Pennsylvania (son of the Presbyterian Neo-Pentecostal leader, James Brown), and Shakarian's oldest son Richard. The 1960 convention in Tulsa, Oklahoma was the scene of the most memorable youth service in the history of the Fellowship. With the main body of the convention meeting in a major ballroom of the Mayo Hotel, about 120 young people were gathered in a smaller room.

As the youth were about to dismiss the service, all 120 were suddenly ''slain in the Spirit,'' and lay sprawled out on the floor for over half an hour while a ''haze of glory'' filled the room. When the elder Shakarian was called to the room to see the sight, he was accompanied by a Messianic Jewish Rabbi. When they saw the well-dressed young people lying on the floor ''in the Spirit,'' the Rabbi pronounced the scene as a modern case of the Old Testament ''Shekinah Glory''. The story of the ''Shekinah'' service entered into the folklore of the movement in years to come.[22]

The next year, 1961, another important miracle happened in Jerusalem during the World Pentecostal Conference which was to affect the future of both Demos Shakarian and the Fellowship. Although he was a registered delegate to the conference, it was, according to Shakarian a "meeting of 4,000 preachers." One evening, while standing in the lobby, Shakarian saw a man who was doubled over with arthritis. He was in the form of a number 7, his upper body parallel with the floor. He was unable to enter the auditorium because he was not a registered delegate. The lady who brought him explained he had come to be healed.

Shakarian not only loaned the man his registration badge, but offered a prayer for his healing. Suddenly the man stood up straight, instantly healed. The joyful screams of the man and lady who brought him electrified the conference. Shakarian left Jerusalem more convinced than ever that laymen could have powerful ministries, even in the presence of thousands of preachers.[23]

The stories of these miracles as well as the rapid growth of FGBMFI in America, which was enthusiastically reported in *Voice,* stirred great interest in other lands. As early as 1955 a new chapter had been chartered in Johannesburg, South Africa as a result of an Oral Roberts crusade in the city. The prime mover in starting this, the first chapter outside America, was Lee Braxton who was helping Roberts in the crusade. This development indicated that Full Gospel Business Men's Fellowship could flourish not only in America, but also far beyond the borders of the United States.[24]

Now, with the Fellowship exploding in the United States, interested people from around the world began to invite FGBMFI to bring its ministry to their own people. The Full Gospel Business Men were willing and ready when the call came.

1. *For news of the growing Los Angeles Chapter see* Voice, *March 1953, p. 13; April, 1953, p. 14; May-June, 1953, p.5.*

2. *Tommy Hicks, "Marvelous Start for the Sioux Falls Chapter," Voice, March 1953, pp. 10-11.*

3. *"International chapters Busy on all Fronts," Voice, September, 1953, pp. 3-4.*

4. *See the "The Story of Demas (sic.) Shakarian and the Full Gospel Business Men's Fellowship," Voice of Healing, August, 1953, pp. 8-10. Although no author was cited, this story was almost certainly written by the Editor, Gordon Lindsay. Cooperation with the healing movement was highlighted with a FGBMFI breakfast held in the Voice of Healing convention in Dallas in 1955. See Voice, October 1955, 29. Harrell contends that the FGBMFI Voice eventually replaced the Voice of Healing as the "coordinating agency of the healing revival."*

5. *Shakarian, "Our Movement is Spreading with Power and Speed," Voice, July-August, 1953, p. 3.*

6. *Sherrill, Happiest People on Earth, pp. 137-8; The story and photos of the headquarter's dedication is given in Shakarian's "Our Movement is Spreading," pp. 1-3.*

7. *Harrell, All Things Are Possible, p. 147.*

8. *Paul B. Fischer, "Our Organization from an Attorney's Standpoint," Voice, Ocotber, 1953, pp. 5-7; The fullest statement of Shakarian's policy toward the churches is given in Voice, November, 1962, p. 19.*

9. *See "A Message of Light Truth and Love," pp. 2-4; and Lee Braxton, "Looking Backward and Forward With Encouragement," Voice, July-August 1953, p. 4.*

10. *Sherrill, Happiest People on Earth, pp. 117-123. The statement on the charismata was given in the Shakarian-Synan interview, February 2, 1988, pp. 2-3.*

11. *Thomas Packard, "Out of Darkness Came Light," Voice, May 1981, pp. 13-15.*

12. *Dr. N. Jerome Stowell and Thomas R. Nickel, "A Scientist Discovers God," Voice, July-August, 1953, pp. 6-9.*

13. 25. *See "God's Mighty Power Manifested at our First Annual Convention," Voice, November, 1953, pp. 8-14. Also see p. 15.*

14. *See Sherrill, Happiest People on Earth, pp. 137-138.*

15. *Ibid., p. 138; "God's Mighty Power Manifest in our First Annual Convention," Voice, November. 1953, pp. 8-14.*

12. Dr. N. Jerome Stowell and Thomas R. Nickel, "A Scientist Discovers God," Voice, July-August, 1953, pp. 6-9.

13. See "God's Mighty Power Manifested at our First Annual Convention," Voice, November, 1953, pp. 8-14. Also see p. 15.

14. See Sherrill, Happiest People on Earth, pp. 137-138.

15. Ibid., p. 138; "God's Mighty Power Manifest in our First Annual Convention," Voice, November, 1953, pp. 8-14.

16. See "New Chapters Arising Throughout Nation," Voice, 1954, p. 11.

17. See Tommy Hicks, "Argentina is Opened to the Full Gospel," Voice, May 1954, pp. 4-5; "Argentina Revival Noted by Doctors," Voice, July-August, 1954, pp. 14-15. A special issue devoted to the Argentinian crusade appeared in the September issue of Voice. See especially Dan L. Thrapp, "The Historic Argentina Revival" pp. 8-10. More information on the Argentina Revival was given in the Hicks obituary, "Closing Time Gentlemen" Voice, April, 1973, pp. 20-21. The 400,000 figure was reported in The Voice of Healing, October, 1954, pp. 8-9.

In his 1956 book, Millions Found Christ (privately printed), Hicks recounted his vision which appears to be the one he received in Shakarian's home. Like Demos' vision, Hicks saw "multitudes" of people beckoning for him to come and minister to them. Then he saw a map of South America which led him ultimately to Argentina. Another of his books, It's Closing Time (N.P. N.D.) chronicled his later campaigns in New Zealand.

18. Demos Shakarian, "Our God is Moving," Voice, July-August, 1954, pp. 3-9.

19. For a report on Nixon see Voice, July-August, 1954, pp. 3-9; also see Richard Nixon, "The Minds and Hearts and Souls of Men," Voice, September, 1954, pp. 4-7. For the Ronald Reagan appearance, see Voice, November, 1966, p. 16.

20. See "From the Editor's Mail," Voice, September, 1954, p. 13.

21. Demos Shakarian, "God is Moving Throughout Our Land," Voice, January, 1955, pp. 4-11.

22. Interview with Demos and Richard Shakarian, May 27, 1992, Costa Mesa, California. For a description of the "Shekinah" service see "I'll Never be the Same Again," Voice, July/August, 1960, pp. 12-25.

23. Shakarian-Synan interview, May 27, 1992. For an account of the healing see Donald Gee, "World Pentecostal Conference Held in Jerusalem," Voice, September, 1961, p. 34.

24. "South Africa Has New FGBM Chapter," Ibid., p. 14

Chapter Six

AN INTERNATIONAL MOVEMENT

*We are called to fulfill a global mission... We see this
vast global movement of laymen comprised of
millions of men, being used mightily of God to bring
this last great harvest through the outpouring of the
Holy Spirit before the return of our Lord Jesus Christ.
—Demos Shakarian, 1984*

Although FGBMFI had its beginnings and developed first in the United States, there was from the beginning an ultimate vision of a worldwide movement made up of men who would lead a "layman's revival" that would shake the world. This global vision was consistently presented in the prophecies given to Shakarian by Hansen and Price, as well as in the "Oriental rug" vision of 1952. Even though the first name adopted by the group was "Full Gospel Business Men of America," this name was short-lived and never took root. In a few months, the official name ended with the word "International".

Even with the foundation of the first overseas chapter in Johannesburg, South Africa in 1955, Shakarian was not excited about the international future of the organization. It was when the first Canadian chapter was formed in Toronto in 1956 that Shakarian felt that the

Fellowship was moving onward beyond the United States. "From then on," he said, "the word 'international' in our name made more sense."[1]

Although the Fellowship continued to experience great growth in the United States throughout the 1950's, its growth overseas was even more remarkable. The international outreach began, as in America, on the trail of the healing evangelists and their crusades. The most unlikely of these was Tommy Hicks who captured the imagination of the religious world with his unexpectedly massive crusade in Buenos Aires, Argentina in 1954. Described by the *Los Angeles Times* as a "pint-sized...gaunt-faced Bible-thumping evangelist from Texas," Hicks saw his crowds increase from 5,000 to 15,000 to 60,000 and ultimately to 200,000 per night. Some even reported crowds as large as 400,000 as multitudes who couldn't get into the stadium filled the nearby streets. The Buenos Aires papers reported that "high officials in the government, including the highest (President Peron) were reported in attendance." During the crusade, Hicks presented Peron with a Bible and a copy of Full Gospel Business Men's *Voice.*[2]

Suddenly Hicks was in demand to hold crusades around the world. In the wake of the publicity surrounding the Argentine crusade, Hicks, with the full support of FGBMFI, journeyed to Russia, Switzerland, Finland, and back to Argentina for a second crusade in 1955. Other crusades in Germany led by William Branham, F.F. Bosworth, and Harold Herman led to a growing European interest in the Fellowship. Everywhere these evangelists traveled, they called for businessmen to meet and form new FGBMFI chapters.[3]

In 1956 new chapters were formed in Toronto, Canada; Calcutta, India; Monterrey, Mexico (after a crusade by Branham); London, England; and Hong Kong, China (after a crusade by A.C. Valdez). Furthermore, by the end of 1958 new chapters had also been formed in Singapore and in Karlsruhe, West Germany. In Latin America, new chapters were formed in Mexico City and Havana, Cuba. The Havana chapter was formed in 1959 after a Shakarian visit with Fidel Castro who said of FGBMFI, "I like what you men are doing."[4]

International growth continued apace with almost every evangelist who ministered abroad. In 1957, an American evangelist by the name of Sam Todd introduced the FGBMFI organization to Korea. Returning to the U.S. he reported that on a recent trip he had organized the first Korean chapters in Kwang-Ju and Kunsan. Tommy Hicks was also busy on the international front, organizing a new chapter in Capetown, South Africa. An "around the world mission" by Miner Arganbright and Thomas Nickel in 1959 brought FGBMFI to six new European and Asian nations including the first Japanese chapters in Kobe and Tokyo. The Fellowship grew so rapidly in Europe, partly due to the massive Holland crusades by T.L. Osborn, that by 1961 the first European convention was conducted in Zurich, Switzerland where 18 nations were represented.[5]

While FGBMFI evangelism usually took place in the context of opening new chapters after major crusades by the healing evangelists, there were several uniquely Full Gospel crusades overseas unlike anything ever seen before. The first one, called "Squadrons," began in 1959 under the inspiration of Irvine Harrison, who in 1957 had been named "Executive Secretary" of the Fellowship. Under this program, Full Gospel lay preachers paid their way to evangelize in Latin America. According to Harrison, the first "Squadron of Commandos" went to Mexico where they served as "shock troops" to "establish footholds and beachheads in the heart of enemy territory." On this first invasion, "multitudes of new converts" were baptized in rivers and streams after being evangelized.[6]

THE AIRLIFTS

Another novel method of spreading the FGBMFI message was the "airlift," a project in which American members chartered airplanes so that hundreds could travel to the far reaches of the world spreading the Full Gospel message. The first airlift project developed after Shakarian received an invitation from President Francois Duvalier to conduct three weeks of meetings in Haiti. Although Duvalier was known to be an "absolute dictator," using torture and secret police to crush his opposition, Rose Shakarian persuaded Demos that Haiti was, after all, a part of the world that needed to be evangelized.[7]

Thus in February, 1960, a planeload of 25 FGBMFI men took off for Haiti. Each of the businessmen paid his own fare and arranged his winter vacation to include the dates of the Haiti mission. The meetings, which were held in the Silvio Cato Stadium in Port Au Prince, exceeded the wildest dreams of the planners, drawing 23,000 persons to the stadium the first night and soon overflowing to 35,000 persons. Despite opposition from voodoo priests, and the dubious support of Duvalier, the campaign continued with increasing force. After the sensational healing of a blind boy, the meetings overflowed the stadium grounds. On the last night in the stadium, over 10,000 persons came forward for salvation. After the three weeks ended, it was estimated that over 100,000 had been saved.[8]

THE LONDON AIRLIFT

As successful as the Haitian crusade turned out to be, the project that caught the fancy of the Fellowship and established the airlift as a primary mode of world evangelization was the London crusade of 1965. The inspiration for this operation was a young Irishman turned Canadian, Ray Barnett, who worked in a travel agency in his hometown of Calgary, Alberta, in western Canada. By 1963, Barnett had founded a chapter of FGBMFI in Calgary and had become obsessed with a vision for a great "world convention" of the Fellowship in London. He also envisioned planeloads of American Full Gospel Business Men landing in London and filling the great halls of the city with Spirit-filled laymen who would "reach thousands of people with the Gospel."9

Barnett shared this vision with Jerry Jensen, who was then serving as editor of *Voice* magazine, during their visit to the famous Banff resort in Canada. After hearing the vision, Jensen became enthused with Barnett's idea of combining an airlift with a "world convention" which would be held in London. To explain the idea to Shakarian, Ray flew to Los Angeles where he and Jerry laid the vision before the president. Although only 15 minutes had been scheduled for the presentation, Shakarian became so interested in the project that the three spent the better part of the day and into the night discussing plans for the event. When he left for the airport the next day, Barnett had been named "Convention Coordinator" for a three-week "London Airlift" and the 1965 "FGBMFI World Convention."10

In a short time Barnett formed a steering committee of British renewal leaders to plan the convention. Members of the committee were the Revs. Michael Harper and Ernest Walton Lewsey, Andy Milliken, and William Thompson. This committee carried out the tremendous task of organizing the local arrangements for the airlift. In the meantime, Barnett chartered three jet planes which in November were filled with 400

FGBMFI members who flew to London for the Convention.

Since there were no other passengers on the planes, the men were free to pray and sing to their hearts' content. On one of the planes, the pilot saw an irregularity in the flight controls but could find no mechanical reason for the problem. When a co-pilot walked back through the plane, he saw the problem immediately. All the passengers were in the rear of the plane worshipping God, causing a dangerous imbalance in the plane. They were ordered politely back to their seats after being warned that otherwise, "they were likely to meet their Maker sooner than envisaged." The crew members were amazed that on all three planes "there was no drinking or smoking, no flirting with the crew, just people praying, singing and praising the Lord." One man received the baptism in the Holy Spirit while they were flying 32,000 feet in the air.[11]

The three weeks that followed amounted to a spiritual blitz of London, as well as other parts of Britain. Just before the arrival of the planes, *The Sunday Express* had carried a full-page article on "the people who speak in a language they do not know." When the Americans arrived, another headline said; "Millionaire Demos brings deliverance to the beatniks of Britain." Throughout the three weeks of the meetings, the British newspapers chronicled the daily activities of the group, especially their ministry to those in the youth drug culture.[12]

Indeed, a major ministry of the airlift was to the drug-addicted beatniks of Soho, a district infamous for its drug and homosexual subculture. Three young converts from the American drug scene: Nicky Cruz, John Giminez and Jack Brown, were brought over to minister to the drug addicts. Of the many who were converted, most were brought to a hotel where International Director George Gardner had rented two rooms to serve as a temporary barbershop. Soon over six inches of hair shorn from the heads of the new converts covered the floors of Gardner's rooms. The news of these events brought news reporters from BBC and Granada news swarming to the hotels to follow the story.[13]

The theme chosen for the London meetings was "From North America to Great Britain...in the Power of the Holy Spirit...Phase One—London—A Convention for Revival." Convention services were in the Westminster Hall and the Royal Albert Hall, the largest and most famous venues in London. After filling Westminster for several days, the convention moved to the Royal Albert for the last day of sessions. Although the hall seated over 7,000 persons, it was filled not once, but twice in one day! Even at that, several thousand persons were unable to get inside the hall. Oral Roberts, who brought the final address, shocked many and thrilled others when he asked all those present to stand and "speak out loud in tongues." For once in its history, the venerable Royal Albert sounded like the upper room in Jerusalem.[14]

In addition to these mass gatherings, the Full Gospel men spent two more weeks in Great Britain holding rallies in several other cities. In the course of the convention, over 100,000 gospel tracts were handed out in the streets. Throughout Britain, Full Gospel Business Men preached on street corners, in rented halls, in barbershops and even in wimpy bars. Some of the speakers who crisscrossed the British Isles were Pat Robertson, Judge Kermit Bradford, and Derek Prince. Nor was this all. After the London convention, various members of the group fanned out in teams to minister in Wales, Ireland, Scotland, Sweden, Italy, Holland, France, and

Spain.[15]

The London Airlift made an indelible impression on Great Britain as well as other nations, and led ultimately to the formation of hundreds of chapters throughout Europe. Unquestionably the airlift technique was a tremendous tool of world evangelization as well as a highly successful method of spreading the FGBMFI organization around the world.[16]

Other airlifts in 1966 took loads of businessmen to the Far East (Honolulu, Hong Kong, Manila, and Tokyo), and to Europe (Sweden, Estonia, Norway, Germany, Finland, Denmark and Holland). An airlift in 1967 brought a planeload to South America (Chile, Ecuador, Bolivia, Argentina, Brazil, and Venezuela). In that same year an airlift brought the FGBMFI message to the war-torn cities of South Vietnam. A 1969 airlift found Full Gospel Business Men in Rome and Jerusalem. These spiritual junkets not only helped to strengthen the Fellowship in those countries, but also gave the American businessmen exposure to other cultures and styles of religious expression.[17]

Three Americans of Scandinavian descent soon took up the cause of the Airlift, and developed it into a major evangelistic tool. They were: Simon Vikse of New York City, Henry Carlson of Chicago, and Enoch Christofferson of Turlock, California. Vikse, a developer and builder from Long Island, had founded the New York City chapter of FGBMFI and was a prime mover in scheduling major evangelistic events in the city. In 1973, Vikse organized an airlift to Norway, the home of his grandparents. Here a strong chapter was organized in Oslo. Over the years, Vikse organized several airlifts to various Scandinavian countries, establishing strong FGBMFI chapters as he went.[18]

A similar ministry was carried out by Henry Carlson, founder of the Chicago chapter of FGBMFI and an

International Director. From 1966 to 1973, Carlson organized and led eight different airlifts to Scandinavia and other parts of Europe. Wherever he went, Carlson also organized FGBMFI chapters. In a real sense, Vikse and Carlson were FGBMFI apostles to northern Europe.[19]

Another Scandinavian American with an "airlift" ministry was Enoch Christoffersen of Turlock, California. An independently wealthy man whose business was raising and processing turkeys, Christoffersen was a tireless and unselfish promoter of the Fellowship. Beginning in 1966, he led several airlifts to the Far East, establishing FGBMFI chapters in many Oriental lands. For over ten years, Christoffersen organized these airlifts and paid most of the costs himself.[20]

Another evangelization technique similar to the airlift was the "Sealift" which was inaugurated in 1975. In this more leisurly type of trip, 160 Full Gospelers in 1976 went to Nassau and Freeport in the Bahamas on the sleek S.S. Emerald Seas where they reportedly "basked in spiritual blessings." It was an opportunity, said tour director Dave Rushton, "to combine business (the Lord's) with sightseeing by distributing copies of *Voice* and speaking in local churches and in a hotel session in Nassau.[21]

VIETNAM AIRLIFT

The war in Vietnam made a Far Eastern airlift of 1967 of special import and even of danger for the 32 men who traveled to that war-torn land. Landing in Saigon, they witnessed to the servicemen on the streets, in the servicemen's center and at the base. To the sound of constant gunfire and nearby bombing raids, the FGBMFI men witnessed about Jesus while handing out tracts and copies of *Voice* magazine. Before being allowed to visit the war zones, the laymen led 65 soldiers to Christ in Saigon. On a tour after leaving Saigon, the war came home to them suddenly when a jeep was blown up a short time before they were to arrive at a speaking engagement.[22]

While in Vietnam, the members of the airlift visited such "hot" war zones as Cam Ranh Bay, Pleiku, as well as the American installations in Saigon. Coming during the dangerous days of the Tet offensive, members of the group were often forced to run for cover or dive into foxholes when they came under enemy fire. During the airlift, Jerry Jensen became convinced that the ultimate problem in Vietnam was spiritual. "Victory or loss in Vietnam is up to the church," he said.[23]

FGBMFI involvement in Vietnam went far beyond the airlift stage in 1967 when Henry Carlson, president of the Chicago chapter envisioned founding a "Christian Center" in South Vietnam for American servicemen. Located in Vung Tau, it was "close enough to hear the distant sound of mortars, but far enough away to provide a few hours of relaxation and Christian fellowship to the men in uniform." For the next few years, *Voice* carried many testimonies from servicemen and the miracles of deliverance they experienced during the war.[24]

The constant fear of terrorist attacks made it difficult for them to travel, especially in the war zones. Welcoming the mission to Vietnam was Army Chaplain Merlin Carothers, author of the best seller, *From Prison to Praise*. In a letter to FGBMFI members, Shakarian characterized the mission as " a true tale of trials, tragedies, and triumphs from the trails, tents, and trenches of torn, tattered, tearful Vietnam." To the soldiers, Shakarian promised to send 100,000 copies of *Voice* each month to Vietnam. Through this trip, members of FGBMFI made their Christian witness in one of the most bewildering and bloody wars of modern times.[25]

The growing international character of the Fellowship was further emphasized in 1964 when the first foreign-language edition of *Voice* appeared in Spanish. Called *La Voz,* this periodical became the first of many non-English editions of the magazine which were to appear over the years. The growth of the ministry in America was also underscored in 1967 with the publication of three new FGBMFI magazines entitled *Vision, Charisma Digest,* and *View.* Indeed, by 1962 the American edition of *Voice* surpassed the 100,000 mark on its way to an all-time high in 1989 of 700,000 readers.[26]

The international ministry of FGBMFI continued to expand throughout the decade of the 1950's and 1960's, largely through the influence of the healing evangelists: Oral Roberts, Tommy Hicks and WIlliam Branham. But in the end, it was the image and example of the businessmen themselves that sold thousands of laymen around the world on the merits of the Fellowship. To be sure, the message of Jesus as Savior, Healer, and Baptizer in the Holy Spirit was the central attraction of the organization. In particular, thousands of pastors and laymen came especially to receive the tongues-attested Pentecostal experience. As such, FGBMFI played a large part in the spread of Pentecostalism into many nations, both developed and undeveloped.

Another major source of new members during the 1960's was the "neo-Pentecostal movement" which was sweeping through the mainline churches not only in the United States but in most other countries of the world. This meant that the membership of the Fellowship varied greatly from nation to nation. For instance, the chapter in Malta, a tiny island nation near Italy, was

made up almost entirely of Roman Catholic charismatics. In the United Kingdom, on the other hand,
Anglicans and free house church members tended to
predominate. When David Barrett was doing research
for his influential *World Christian Encyclopedia* in
1980, he found that the major gathering of Christians in
such Islamic nations as Kuwait and Saudia Arabia were
Full Gospel Business Men who served the western business communities.

Leaders of the European Pentecostal movement
were favorably impressed with the work of the Fellowship, especially after the London Airlift. In 1971, Lewi
Pethrus, pastor of the largest free church in Europe, the
huge Filadelphia Pentecostal church in Stockholm, said
of FGBMFI:

> "All believers should be priests and...for this
> reason, I praise God for FGBMFI. It is an instru-
> ment to open the churches to the charismatic
> renewal."[27]

High praise of Full Gospel Business Men was also
expressed by Donald Gee, the highly respected English
Pentecostal Leader who edited *Pentecost,* the only
worldwide voice of the movement. In a letter to *Voice*
in 1955, he stated that he found the periodical an "in-
creasingly interesting and inspiring periodical." He further added, "It seems to me as though the Spirit of God
is in this FGBMF, and I wish you every success."[28]

In addition to the obvious spiritual attractiveness
of the Fellowship, there was an economic and social
appeal that was extremely attractive to the poor and
oppressed people who heard the Gospel from men
who were prosperous as well as spiritual. The idea that
those men who serve the Lord in the power of the Holy
Spirit, who work hard and live honestly, will prosper
like the men of FGBMFI, was an extremely attractive
ideal to masses of the world's poor people who were

struggling for a better life.

In the end, it was the attraction of Jesus, coupled with the ideal of the American dream of prosperity for those who serve the Lord, that fueled the engine of the FGBMFI expansion around the world. The success of the Fellowship was evident in the reports given in the World Convention of 1963, celebrating the first decade of its existence. According to David Harrell:

> The growth of the Fellowship in the 1960's and 1970's was startling. By the mid 1960's it had established three hundred chapters with approximately 100,000 members...and each issue of *Voice* carried news of new local chapters and increasing membership.[29]

The tenth anniversary convention of the Fellowship convened in Fresno, California in October, 1963 ending what Shakarian called "A Decade of Destiny." That destiny included planting the FGBMFI banner throughout America and in dozens of nations outside the United States. Indeed, Shakarian had become "the shepherd of a huge charismatic flock."[30] In 1963, this flock included seven members of an "Executive Committee," eight "Regional Directors," a "Board" of 25 additional members, and nine "Foreign Directors."[31]

The growth of the Fellowship during the 1960's meant that the word "International" in the name was not an empty word. Demos' vision of "millions and millions of men with raised heads and hands lifted towards heaven" was now becoming a reality.[32]

---

1. *Sherrill,* Happiest People on Earth, *p.10.*

2. See "The Historic Argentina Revival," pp. 4-5; "The Greatest Revival in All History," Voice, February-May, 1955, pp.4-7. For the 400,000 figure, see Tommy Hicks interview with Gordon Lindsay entitled "400,000 in Single Service," in The Voice of Healing, August, 1954, pp. 19-30.

3. See Voice, *October, 1955, pp. 3-18; January, 1956, pp. 10-16.*

4. The beginnings of the British FGBMFI is told in Val Fotherby's Catching the Vision: A British Sequel to The Happiest People on Earth—The FGBMFI Story. *(Eastbourne, East Sussex: Kingsway Press, 1989), although no mention is made of the 1956 organization; also see* Voice, *June, 1956, p. 3 for news of the 1956 London chapter. For the beginning of the Hong Kong chapter see* Voice, *March, 1956, p. 3; for the Calcutta chapter,* Voice, *May 1956, p. 3. The Cuban story is in* Voice, *March, 1959, pp. 19-21.*

5. See Voice, *August, 1957, pp. 17-22 (Capetown and Korea); "Phenomenal Success of FGBMFI in Japan,"* Voice, *January 1959, pp. 3-8. The story of the Zurich Convention is reported in* Voice, *May, 1961, pp. 18-19. The report of Osborn's massive Netherlands crusade with photos of 100,000 people in attendance was reported in William A. Caldwell, "One of the Greatest Spiritual Awakenings of all Time,"* Voice, *April, 1959, pp. 12-16.*

6. Irvine J. Harrison, "Latin America Needs the Peace of God," Voice, *December, 1959, pp. 16-19.*

7. The Haitian crusade was reported in Sherrill's Happiest People on Earth, *pp. 151-160.*

8. See Irvine Harrison "Report of the Caribbean Crusade", in Voice, *March, 1960, pp. 20-23.*

9. The full story of the London airlift is related in Fotherby's Catching the Vision, *pp. 21-52.*

10. Ibid., *pp. 22-23.*

11. Ibid., *pp. 27-28.*

12. Ibid., *pp. 31-32.*

13. Ibid., *pp. 32-33.*

14. Ibid., *pp. 36-38.*

15. Ibid., *p. 40.*

16. See the booklet Airlift to London *(FGBMFI publication), 1966, pp. 1-64; Fotherby,* Catching the Vision, *pp. 21-42; also* Voice, *January-February, 1966, pp. 3-5, 23.*

17. For reports on other airlifts see: Voice, *November, 1966, pp. 8-15 (the Far East); December, 1966, pp. 8-17, 22 (Europe); January-February, 1968, pp. 8-15, 22-27 (South America); October, 1969, pp. 34-36 (Jerusalem). For the stories on the Vietnam airlift see the special military edition published in November 1967, pp. 8-17.*

18. See Simon Vikse, "Man of Two Countries," Voice, *November 1974, pp. 2-8.*

19. Henry Carlson, "Man With a Mission," Voice, *October, 1973, pp. 2-25.*

20. See *"Far East Airlift,"* Voice, *November, 1966, pp.9-14, and Enoch Christoffersen, "...Remember Thy Creator..."* Voice, *January/February, 1969, pp. 4-7, 22-25, 35.*

21. See Voice, *June 1976, p. 40.*

22. See *"Far East Airlift,"* Voice, *November, 1967, pp. 8-17. Also see Jerry Jensen, "Vietnam, You Were There,"* Voice, *April, 1967, pp. 4-15.*

23. For more on the airlift, see Jerry Jensen, *"Vietnam: Laymen Minister to the Military,"* Acts, *July-August, 1967, pp. 5-7.*

24. *"A Vision for Viet Nam,"* Voice, *July/August, 1968, pp. 25-27.*

25. *Demos Shakarian letter entitled, "The Voice of Vietnam."*

26. For the La Voz announcement see Voice, *June, 1969, p. 3; For the Seattle Convention and circulation figures see* Voice, *September, 1962, pp. 1-17.*

27. See Voice, *March 1971, p. 11.*

28. See the letter from Donald Gee in Voice, *April, 1955, p. 20.*

29. *Harrell,* All Things Are Possible, *p. 147. Also see John T. Nichol,* Pentecostalism *(New York: Harper & Row, 1966), pp. 241-242.*

30. *William C. Armstrong, "A Decade of Destiny,"* Voice, *October, 1963, pp. 4-7.*

31. See *"International Board of Directors,"* Voice, *October, 1963, p. 3.*

32. *Sherrill,* Happiest People on Earth, *pp. 133-134.*

▲ *Demos and his father Isaac in front of the Shakarian home in Downey, California.*

The original Shakarian home on ▶ Boston Ave. in Los Angeles. Early Armenian services were conducted here.

▼ *This drive-in unit was located at the headquarters of Reliance Dairies.*

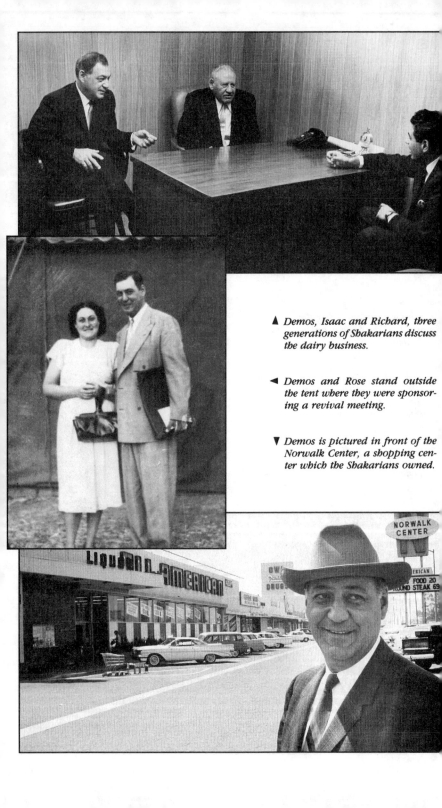

▲ *Demos, Isaac and Richard, three generations of Shakarians discuss the dairy business.*

◄ *Demos and Rose stand outside the tent where they were sponsoring a revival meeting.*

▼ *Demos is pictured in front of the Norwalk Center, a shopping center which the Shakarians owned.*

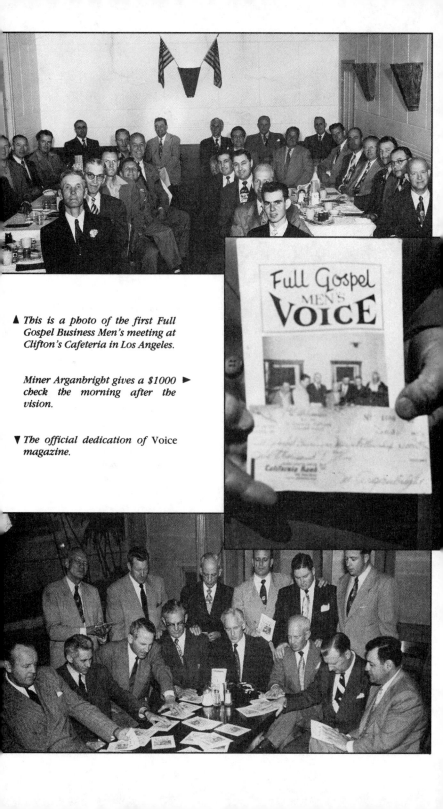

▲ *This is a photo of the first Full Gospel Business Men's meeting at Clifton's Cafeteria in Los Angeles.*

Miner Arganbright gives a $1000 ► *check the morning after the vision.*

▼ *The official dedication of* Voice *magazine.*

▲ *Attorney Paul Fisher (left) discusses the Constitution and By-Laws for the Fellowship with Secretary Earl Draper and President Demos Shakarian.*

◄ *Demos signs the Articles of Incorporation as attorney Fisher looks on.*

▼ *Louis Scoma, Jack Coe and Demos Shakarian at Washington, D.C. convention.*

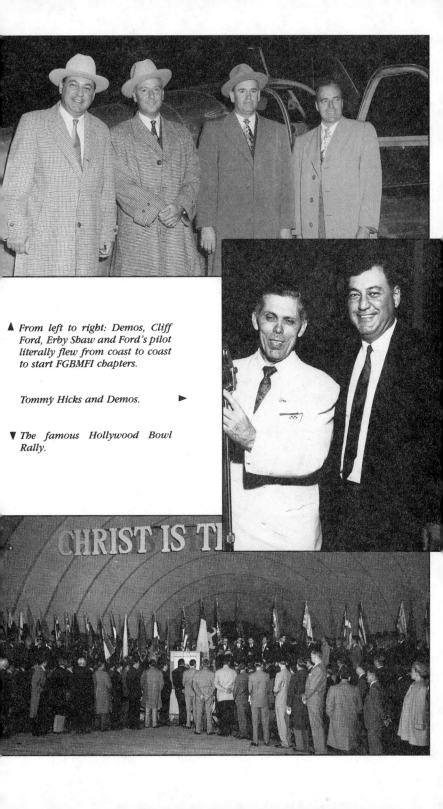

▲ From left to right: Demos, Cliff Ford, Erby Shaw and Ford's pilot literally flew from coast to coast to start FGBMFI chapters.

Tommy Hicks and Demos. ►

▼ The famous Hollywood Bowl Rally.

CHRIST IS TH

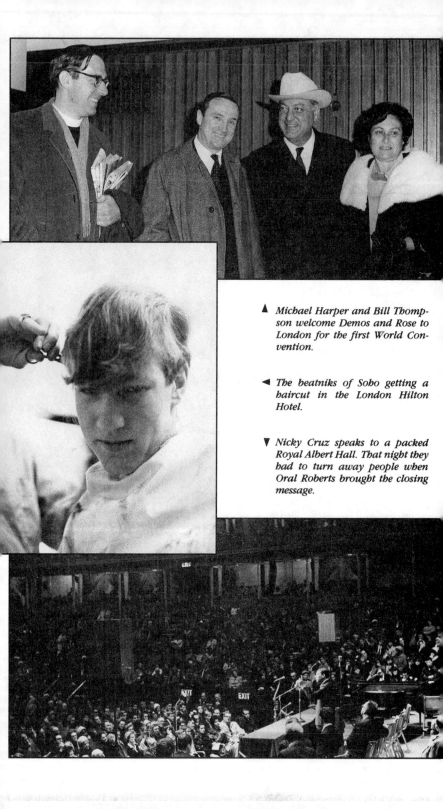

▲ *Michael Harper and Bill Thompson welcome Demos and Rose to London for the first World Convention.*

◄ *The beatniks of Soho getting a haircut in the London Hilton Hotel.*

▼ *Nicky Cruz speaks to a packed Royal Albert Hall. That night they had to turn away people when Oral Roberts brought the closing message.*

▲ Jerry Jensen leads songs at the London convention session in the Hilton Hotel. Following the convention the men went all over Europe sharing their testimonies.

During the Scandinavian airlift ▶ Demos talks with Lewi Pethrus, pastor of the huge Filadelphia Church in Stockholm.

▼ Sheldon Clements and Jerry Jensen prepare to fly out to the combat zone with a helicopter crew during the Vietnam Airlift.

▲ *Demos talks over plans for the new headquarters building with contractor T.L. Whaley.*

◄ *Oral Roberts speaks at the dedication of the new headquarters.*

▼ *FGBMFI headquarters building.*

Chapter Seven

FGBMFI—
AN ECUMENICAL FORCE

*It's always nice to be back with God's Ballroom
Saints. I want you to know that my feeling has never
changed; I consider FGBMFI to be the greatest single
move of the Holy Spirit in the world today.*
—Oral Roberts, 1974

Not only did Full Gospel Business Men spread beyond the geographical bounds of the United States in the 1960's, but also far beyond its original Pentecostal base into the world of the mainline churches. The seeds of this new penetration were planted when Dennis Bennett, an Episcopalian, spoke in tongues in 1960 and was allowed to remain in his denomination. This opened a new era not only for the churches but for FGBMFI as well. Like Bennett, many other mainline ministers had spoken in tongues before 1960, but few had escaped persecution and excommunication from their churches.[1]

FGBMFI soon became the major platform and occasional haven for these new preachers who were quickly dubbed "neo-Pentecostals" by the religious press. Just as the healing evangelists found a home in Full Gospel Business Men's Fellowship in the 1950's, in like manner these "new" Pentecostals were also welcomed with open arms. Throughout the 1960's the pages of *Voice* were filled with news of Pentecostal renewal in the mainline churches. Many of these new Pentecostals became featured speakers on both the local chapter and national convention speaking circuits. Some of the early neo-Pentecostals featured in FGBMFI circles were Presbyterians James Brown and Brick Bradford: Lutherans Larry Christenson and Herbert Mjorud: as well as Baptists Charles Simpson, John Osteen, and Pat Robertson. Also featured were Methodist evangelist Tommy Tyson, and Dutch Reformed pastor Harald Bredesen.[2]

THE NEO-PENTECOSTALS

Life for some of these "neo's" was particularly difficult. In some cases, the offerings received in FGBMFI meetings made the difference between survival and poverty. Brick Bradford, while undergoing judicial proceedings from the Oklahoma Indian Nations Presbytery, survived for several years on the free-will offerings of local Pentecostal churches and his income from speaking on the Full Gospel circuit. Many others shared the same experience.[3]

It was not always easy for some people from mainline denominational backgrounds to attend FGBMFI meetings. The fear of criticism was especially real for many people, although the spiritual attraction of the chapter meetings was often overwhelming. One couple from Texas went to local meetings despite a "nameless fear" of losing social status from their association with Full Gospel Business Men. Coming to the chapter meetings, explained Claude Woods, "was almost as if we were sneaking into a liquor store or an x-rated movie." Yet the Woods, like thousands of others, found the peace they were seeking in the chapter meetings.[4]

As the number of neo-Pentecostals increased, Shakarian was careful to emphasize that FGBMFI was not a substitute denomination. He consistently counseled them to stay in their churches and "bloom where you are planted." In 1974 he emphasized the interdenominational nature of the Fellowship by saying:

> "We are not interested in starting new churches ...people should not leave the church after receiving the baptism in the Holy Spirit...tithes should not be sent to FGBMFI...we need the church...we are laborers together."[5]

According to Shakarian, the Fellowship was making an evangelistic contribution that the churches, as necessary as they were, could not make. "I feel," he wrote in 1962, "that God has shown us a way to reach men that cannot be reached in any other way...we are reaching with this dynamic message of the Holy Spirit into the denominational churches. It is spreading like wildfire." He furthermore saw the unique role played by the Fellowship in the rapidly growing neo-Pentecostal movement:

> "You can trace the breakthrough of the denominational churches receiving the Holy Spirit as a direct result of FGBMFI testimonies in hotels... all over America...they feel the marvelous presence of God here...not only do they feel it, but they get hungry for God."[6]

CHARISMATIC LEADERSHIP

In support of the growing neo-Pentecostal movement, FGBMFI adopted two early strategies. The first was the publication of a series of booklets promoting the renewal in the various denominations. In 1963 the first one appeared under the title, *Baptists and the Baptism in the Holy Spirit,* which consisted mainly of testimonies previously published in *Voice* magazine.

Following this were others devoted to the Methodists (1963), the Episcopalians (1964) and the Catholics (1968). Another series appeared from 1971 to 1975 entitled *Acts of the Holy Spirit.* These were devoted to Methodists, Episcopalians, Catholics, Nazarenes, Lutherans, Disciples of Christ, and the Churches of Christ. Another series related the baptism in the Holy Spirit to attorneys, physicians, the military, and educators.[7]

The second project was the calling of a special conference of pastors and professors to discuss "the Charismatic Revival." Meeting in New York City in November of 1963, this theological symposium drew over 170 teachers, pastors, researchers and writers from 30 colleges, seminaries, and universities. These gathered to hear such speakers as Howard Ervin, James Brown, Dennis Bennett, Harald Bredesen, and Leonard Evans. These speakers discussed the growth of the renewal in the mainline churches and offered guidance to others who were entering into the charismatic dimension. They also grappled with the theological implications of the baptism in the Holy Spirit in other traditions. According to Jerry Jensen, these speakers and conferees represented "the nation's intellectual cream" of charismatic leadership. This was one of the earliest ecumenical academic charismatic conferences ever held. It was also one of the first conferences to specifically use the term "charismatic."[8]

CATHOLIC RENEWAL

The policy of flexibility and support for the Protestant neo-Pentecostal movement continued when a Pentecostal renewal unexpectedly broke out in the Roman Catholic Church in 1967. Beginning in Pittsburgh with a group of theology professors and students, the movement among Catholics spread rapidly to the University of Michigan in Ann Arbor and to the campus of Notre Dame University in South Bend, Indiana. It was in South Bend that FGBMFI became directly involved with the Catholic movement.[9]

Upon hearing about the outbreak of glossolalia and other gifts of the Spirit in Pittsburgh, a group of graduate theology students at Notre Dame began to seek someone in the city who could help them in their search for the baptism in the Holy Spirit. The person they found was Ray Bullard, president of the South Bend chapter of FGBMFI and a janitor in a local public school. On March 13, 1967, Bullard invited a group of young students to a meeting in the basement of his home in nearby Mishawaka. Here such future leaders of the Catholic Charismatic renewal as Kevin Ranaghan, Bert Ghezzi, and Kerry Koller, spoke in tongues for the first time. Their decision to remain in the Catholic church, which was made in Bullard's basement prayer room, became the launching pad for the "People of Praise" charismatic community in South Bend, and the Notre Dame conferences which began in 1967.[10]

Soon Roman Catholic speakers were in evidence at chapter meetings and national and international FGBMFI conventions around the world. Among these were Kevin Ranaghan, Professor Edward O'Connor of Notre Dame University, Father John Bertolucci, and Charlie Osborne, a fiery Catholic layman. An early sign of support was a special issue of *Voice* dedicated to the Catholic movement which appeared in September of 1971. Unlike most Pentecostal churches and Pentecostal para-church groups, FGBMFI was highly successful in integrating the Catholics into their organization, and with a surprising ease.[11]

Not only did the Fellowship feature mainline Protestant and Catholic speakers in chapters and conferences, but it also succeeded to a remarkable degree in integrating men from many church backgrounds into the local chapters. People from all churches not only joined as members, but served as leaders in the local chapters. A 1979 study of a local chapter in Virginia indicated the broad range of membership throughout the organization. The denominational makeup of this chapter was as follows; Catholic 3%: Episcopal 8%: Lutheran 15%: Presbyterian 25%: United Church of Christ 2%: United Methodist 21%: Baptist 9%: Church of the Brethren 6%: Mennonite 10%: Pentecostal 3%.[12]

The format of the typical chapter and convention meeting encouraged a warm fellowship across denominational lines and offered an emotional release which most mainline church members did not receive in their local churches. While at first, many people were turned off by what they saw in a chapter meeting, most soon entered into the spirit of the meetings and came to enjoy the freedom of expressive worship and praise that they found there. Although FGBMFI was most certainly not a new denomination, it served that function for many people who were converted or healed in the chapter meetings. Whatever happened in local chapters was multiplied in the conventions which by the mid-1970's were attracting up to 20,000 people.

CONVENTION HIGHLIGHTS

The hotel ballrooms provided a "dignified setting" which made it easier for mainline "neo-Pentecostals" to enter into the Pentecostal experience. Indeed, the FGBMFI meetings not only indicated that many "old-line" Pentecostals were entering the middle class, but that multitudes of prosperous and well-educated people in the mainline churches were more open to charismatic worship and experience than anyone had imagined.[13]

The atmosphere of the hotel ballroom had a mystique all its own that proved to be extremely attractive to those who came. For many old-line Pentecostals, FGBMFI meetings were their first time to see the insides of luxury hotels and ballrooms. In describing the facilities of the 1957 convention in Chicago, the editor of *Voice* waxed eloquent:

> "Here is the Grand Crystal Ballroom of the Sherman Hotel, the headquarters hotel of the FGBMFI convention. The great auditorium seats 2,000 persons. Hung with crystal chandeliers, sparkling above beautifully decorated balconies, the empire splendor provides a fitting atmosphere for a convention honoring the King of Kings!"[14]

One of the most descriptive accounts of a convention meeting was given by John Sherrill, a senior editor of *Guideposts* magazine, in his 1964 book, *They Speak With Other Tongues:*

> On the platform at the end of the room sat two dozen business and professional men. Some, I was told, had flown across the country to attend the meeting; one had come in his own private plane.
>
> While we were finishing our coffee, one of these men stood up and called out the name of a song. Everyone joined in, loud lusty and wonderful...By the middle of the second song a woman at the next table was weeping...Soon some of the men on the platform were unabashedly bringing out their handkerchiefs...
>
> As the music continued, several people at the tables began to "sing in the Spirit." Soon the whole room was singing a complicated harmony-without-score, created spontaneously. It was eerie but extraordinarily beautiful...harmo-

nies and counterharmonies wove in and out of each other.

By now tears were flowing without restraint all around the room. A weathered, stone faced man near us raised calloused hands and sang out "Praise the Lord!" An elderly woman two tables away stood up and began to dance a little jig. No one paid her the slightest attention. Except me, that is."[15]

After this demonstration of emotional power, Demos Shakarian came forward to lead the business meeting for the night. To Sherrill's astonishment, and "relief" the business "was over in five minutes." After a prayer, a preacher came forward to deliver an impassioned sermon. Sherrill was greatly impressed by the variety of churches represented. "There were Episcopalians, Methodists, Baptists, Presbyterians, (and) Lutherans."

Like many others before him and after him, Sherrill was baptized in the Holy Spirit and spoke in tongues at the convention. For him "Room 405," where he received his own personal pentecost with a few friends gathered for prayer, became forever afterwards an important part of his personal spiritual pilgrimage.[16]

Occasionally there were miraculous things that happened in the ballroom meetings of the Fellowship. Although speaking in tongues was common in most meetings, at least once, Shakarian was credited with speaking in zenoglossolalia, (i.e., a known earthly language unknown to the speaker.) In a 1968 meeting of the Beverly Hills chapter, a linguist was present by the name of Donald Liedmann. He reported hearing Shakarian "praying in ancient Aramaic—the language that Jesus had spoken. And he was saying:

"Dear Lord, I thank You for the years I have

been privileged to serve You. Forgive me Lord
for the shortcomings that I have, and let me
serve You even if I am a little man."[17]

The most widely heralded "miracle" connected
with FGBMFI was that of the "Halo over the Hilton"
which occurred during the July 1976 FGBMFI Convention in San Francisco. According to many eyewitnesses,
a rainbow-colored halo appeared over the hotel on July
7, causing a sense of awe and led at least one witness to
become a converted and sanctified Christian. According to Richard Minasian:

"On Friday, July 7, people began talking about a
'halo' which had appeared above the hotel
about noon and was now well into its second
hour. I went outside and looked. Sure enough—
there was a complete rainbow-hued circle over
the hotel in the semi-cloudy sky. It was not
raining, and no rain clouds were visible..." A
man standing nearby said, "Can anyone dis-
believe after this?"[18]

This was not the only instance of uncreated light
to be reported in FGBMFI circles. Members of the Fellowship were also excited by the reports and photos of
another "halo" that appeared over the head of William
Branham while he was speaking in a hotel meeting in
Lausanne, Switzerland in August of 1955. Photos of the
light were run in *Voice* along with reports of
Branham's 1955 German and Swiss crusades.[19]

GOD'S BALLROOM SAINTS

It was in 1974 that Oral Roberts tagged the
FGBMFI people as "God's Ballroom Saints." Although
this name never stuck, it did describe the ambiance of
the movement that attracted so many people of various
cultural and denominational backgrounds. FGBMFI

meetings also became major "tarrying rooms" for those who were seeking the baptism in the Holy Spirit, although few tarried long to receive "the baptism" in the highly-charged hotel atmosphere. When Roberts founded his university in 1965, he enforced a rule that required all faculty members to have received the baptism in the Holy Spirit with the sign of speaking in tongues. Since it was easier for professors to receive the experience in FGBMFI meetings, he had a policy of sending difficult cases to Full Gospel conventions. According to Roberts, they all came back speaking in tongues.[20]

A case in point was that of Bill Jernigan, a librarian at Oral Roberts University who came to the University from a Nazarene background. Perhaps because of that fact, he experienced difficulty in releasing his "prayer language." In 1965, Roberts sent Jernigan to an FGBMFI convention in Phoenix, Arizona where he received the glossolalic experience and returned to serve for the next quarter century as head of the ORU Learning Resources Center. A second important ORU professor was Howard Ervin, the influential biblical scholar, who was baptized in the Holy Spirit at an FGBMFI convention in Miami. Indeed, Roberts claimed that fully one-fourth of his founding faculty received their tongues experience in Full Gospel meetings.[21]

Over the years, thousands of ministers and laymen from all types of backgrounds received their Pentecostal baptism in the Holy Spirit in a fashion similar to that of Jernigan. One of the more important pastors to experience tongues in a Full Gospel Business Men's convention was Jamie Buckingham, pastor of a Southern Baptist congregation in Melbourne, Florida. After being convinced of the reality of the baptism in the Holy Spirit, he traveled to Washington, D.C. to attend an FGBMFI convention. After speaking in tongues in

Washington, he moved on to pastor the Tabernacle Church in Melbourne and to become an influential writer of books and articles. His major work was as editor of *Ministries Today* magazine, and columnist for *Charisma* magazine.[22]

The stories of Jernigan Ervin and Buckingham were typical of a whole generation of ministers from all denominations who were turned on to the Holy Spirit at Full Gospel Business Men's functions. In turn, many of them became zealous missionaries to their friends, inviting them to other FGBMFI meetings where they in turn received the Pentecostal experience.

1. Dennis Bennett, Nine O'Clock in the Morning *(Plainfield, N.J; Logos Press, 1970), pp. 15-21. Also see Vinson Synan,* In the Latter Days, *pp. 90-93.*

2. Many "neo-Pentecostals" were featured in Voice *as well as in the chapter and convention meetings of the Fellowship. Articles by or about the following were carried in* Voice: *James Brown, July-August, 1961, pp. 3-11; Herbert Mjorud, April, 1964, pp. 24-27; John Osteen, October, 1959, p. 26.; and Pat Robertson, April, 1964, pp. 9-11.*

3. Brick Bradford, personal interview with the author, December 6, 1985. Also see Vinson Synan, Twentieth Century Pentecostal Explosion *(Altamonte Springs, Florida; Creation House, 1987), pp. 159-172.*

4. Claude Woods, "A Nameless Fear," Voice, *November 1983, pp. 24-27.*

5. Shakarian, "We are not Interested in Starting New Churches," Voice, *November, 1974, pp. 29-30.*

6. See Voice, *November, 1962, p. 19.*

7. Denominational Booklets:
   Baptist and the Baptism in the Holy Spirit, *1963.*
   Methodists and the Baptism in the Holy Spirit, *1963.*
   Presbyterians and the Baptism in the Holy Spirit, *1963.*
   Episcopalians and the Baptism in the Holy Spirit, *1963.*
   Catholics and the Baptism in the Holy Spirit, *1968.*
   Acts of the Holy Spirit Among the Baptists Today, *1971.*
   Acts of the Holy Spirit Among the United Methodists Today, *1971.*
   Acts of the Holy Spirit Among the Church of Christ Today, *1971.*
   Acts of the Holy Spirit Among the Presbyterians Today, *1972.*
   Acts of the Holy Spirit Among the Nazarenes Today, *1973.*

Acts of the Holy Spirit Among the Catholics Today, *1974*.

Acts of the Holy Spirit Among the Disciples of Christ Today, *1974*.

Acts of the Holy Spirit Among the Lutherans Today, *1975*.

Professional Booklets:

Attorney's Evidence on the Baptism in the Holy Spirit, *1965*.

Physicians Examine the Baptism in the Holy Spirit, *1967*.

Voices of the Military, *1969*.

A Sure Cure; Acts of the Holy Spirit Within the Medical Profession Today, *1976*.

God and the Lawman, *1972*.

The Scholarship of the Spirit; the Acts of the Holy Spirit Among Educators Today, *1977*.

8. For a report on the New York Seminar see Jerry Jensen, "FGBMFI Views the Charismatic Renewal" Voice, *December, 1963, pp. 10-12; 20. The results of the seminar were edited by Jerry Jensen in* The New Pentecost: Charismatic Revival Seminar Report *(Los Angeles; FGBMFI), 1964. A later book about Pentecostal scholarship appeared in 1977 and was entitled* The Scholarship of the Spirit: The Acts of the Holy Spirit Among Educators Today *(Costa Mesa, California; FGBMFI, 1977).*

9. The best early accounts of the Notre Dame meeting can be found in Kevin and Dorothy Ranaghan's Catholic Pentecostals *(New York; Paulist Press, 1969), pp. 6-16, 41; and Edward O'Connor's* The Pentecostal Movement in the Catholic Church *(Notre Dame, Indiana; Ave Maria Press, 1971), pp.24-47. Also see Vinson Synan* In the Latter Days, *pp. 97-118.*

10. Kevin Ranaghan, "Dedication Under the Dome," Voice, *October 1967, pp. 8-30. The September 1971 issue of* Voice *was given over to coverage of the Catholic movement, which was called "the Gentle Revolution." Many stories and photos chronicled the story of Bullard's involvement with the Notre Dame Catholics.*

11. Articles in Voice *by or about Catholic Charismatic leaders include: Edward O'Connor, July-August, 1967, pp.. 25-29; Bert Ghezzi, October, 1967, Jim Cavnar, September, 1971, pp. 8-14, 34-36; Charlie Osborne December, 1988, pp. 2-8.*

12. See Cecil David Bradford, Neo-Pentecostalism: A Sociological Assessment *(Washington, D.C.; University Press of America, 1979), p. 15.*

13. Bradfield, Ibid., *pp. 13-66. This study traced the evolution of Fellowship members from a "deprivation" culture to a middle class ethos "beyond deprivation."*

14. See "Fellowship's Greatest Convention is Expected," Voice, *July, 1957, p. 15.*

15. John L. Sherrill, They Speak With Other Tongues *(Old Tappan, N.J.; Chosen Books, 1964, 1985 revision), pp. 133-136.*

16. Ibid., *p. 135. Sherrill's tongues experience became a model for the thousands of persons who received the baptism in the Holy Spirit at FGBMFI conventions. This book became a major factor in the spread of the movement to professional people like himself. See especially pp. 136-141.*

17. *David Liedmann, "A New Covenant,"* Voice, *Jan.-Feb. 1970, p. 12.*

18. *Richard C. Minasian, "Signs and Wonders,"* Voice, *September, 1976, pp. 2-8.*

19. *F.F. Bosworth, "Branham Meetings in Germany and Switzerland,"* Voice, *September, 1955, pp. 3-11. According to Miner Arganbright who took the photos, "The time was around 11 o'clock and no artificial lighting was used, neither floodlight nor flashlight...the glory of the Lord began to appear over Branham's head as shown in this photograph. See pp. 3-4.*

20. *Roberts-Synan interview, p. 33-34; Oral Roberts, "God's Ballroom Saints",* Voice, *November, 1974, p. 19. For the ORU policy on the baptism in the Holy Spirit and the gift of tongues, see Oral Roberts,* My Twenty Years of A Miracle Ministry *(Tulsa; Oral Roberts ministry, 1967), pp. 72-75.*

21. *Bill Jernigan, personal interview with the author, April 22, 1992, Tulsa, Oklahoma 1992. Synan-Roberts interview, p. 39.*

22. *See "Prophet with a Pen,"* Charisma, *April 1992, pp. 27-31.*

Chapter Eight

ON THE HEIGHTS

"Welcome Full Gospel Business Men...
Dancing Nitely"
—Hotel sign in Long Beach, California

Having espoused the cause of the charismatic movement in the mainline churches, after 1960 FGBMFI became the principal platform and clearing house for the movement for the next two decades. Riding the crest of the charismatic wave, the Fellowship experienced continued growth and influence during the decade of the 1970's and well into the 1980's. There developed during these years a direct relationship in which each wave of renewal in the churches spilled over into the Fellowship, while growth in the Fellowship spilled over into the churches. The attention and emphasis of the movement gradually changed from the healing crusades to the charismatic movement in the mainline churches.

Throughout the early period of the Fellowship's development, Shakarian had relied on the help of the healing evangelists, especially Oral Roberts, Tommy Hicks, William Branham, and Jack Coe. Except for Roberts, this early coterie of helpers dropped off the scene one by one through death; Jack Coe in 1956, William Branham in 1965, and Tommy Hicks in 1973. Oral Roberts, however, has been a constant source of inspiration and leadership throughout the entire forty year history of the Fellowship.[1]

ORAL ROBERTS UNIVERSITY

It was Roberts, who in 1965, founded the major educational institution produced by the Pentecostal/charismatic movement, Oral Roberts University (ORU) in Tulsa, Oklahoma. From the very first, Roberts had played a major role in founding and leading FGBMFI. After the death of Charles Price, Roberts became the prime personal spiritual mentor of Shakarian and over the years played a role somewhat akin to being the national "chaplain" to the Fellowship. Outside of Shakarian, Roberts played the longest and most influential role in the history of the Fellowship. Also, Lee Braxton, who for much of this time was Roberts' right-hand man, also served as Vice-President of FGBMFI and a right-hand man to Shakarian.[2]

When Roberts announced plans for his new university in 1961, Lee Braxton was immediately asked to serve as Chairman of the Board of Regents while Shakarian was asked to serve as one of the founding trustees. So many other FGBMFI leaders were chosen to serve on the various ORU Boards that the two institutions formed a virtual "interlocking directorate." As the university developed, there was an almost symbiotic relationship between Shakarian and Roberts and their multitude of followers. When the University went into operation in 1965, it relied heavily on FGBMFI leaders for expertise and financial support. From the very beginning and through the subsequent years, Shakarian strongly supported the university in all the stages of its development. In fact two of the first buildings on campus when the university opened were named Shakarian Hall and Braxton Hall.[3]

When ORU was dedicated in 1967, *Voice* ran a cover story of the ceremony entitled, "Ecumenical Education" carrying a photo of Oral Roberts and Billy Graham dedicating the university on the cover. Other photos showed some of the 20,000 persons gathered on the campus for the event. The platform erected for the ritual was flanked by Shakarian and Braxton Halls. Much of the later success of the university, especially in the area of finances, could be credited to the close relationship Roberts had cultivated with the Fellowship since the founding of the first chapter in Los Angeles in 1951.[4]

SIGNS OF GROWTH

The founding of Oral Roberts University paralleled an extraordinary period of growth for FGBMFI and the charismatic renewal movement in general. Much of the Fellowship's growth was fueled by the explosive influence of *Voice* which expanded greatly during the 1960's and 1970's. Some issues of *Voice* were in such demand that reprints were ordered. For instance, the edition on Dennis Bennett required a reprint of 9,000 copies to fulfill the flood of requests for extra copies.[5]

The growth of *Voice* was accelerated under Jerry Jensen who succeeded Nickel in the Fall of 1962. When Jensen took over, the subscription list stood at 40,000. When he completed his first period as editor in 1969, the number had mushroomed to 500,000. The reason for this growth, according to Jensen, was the charismatic movement in the mainline churches. "*Voice* crested with the charismatic movement," he said. During the 1970's when many local churches sent their entire mailing lists to be added to the rolls. Throughout its history, *Voice* paid for itself and was never sent out free. Most chapters order bulk mailings which were then used as a means of outreach.[6]

Over the years, interested members took it on themselves to buy and distribute thousands of copies of *Voice* as part of their own personal ministries. The largest case was that of John Paju from Ukiah, California who in 1989 ordered and distributed over 100,000 copies through his local chapter. According to Jerry Jensen, Paju "saturated" his community with copies of *Voice*.

Another gauge of the Fellowship's growth was the dramatic increase in convention registrations in the 1970's. In 1972, the attendance at the World Convention was only 6,000 persons. But by 1975 in Anaheim, the number had increased to over 15,000 in daily attendance. This trend continued through the 1978 "Silver Anniversary" convention in Anaheim where no less than 25,000 came to celebrate the first twenty five years of the Fellowship. Similar growth was experienced in the regional and local conventions and chapter meetings. A high point came in 1974 at the Washington, D.C. Regional Convention where 18,000 persons registered. At one point Shakarian boasted that, with 140 conventions annually in America, FGBMFI was one of the top ten renters of hotel and convention space in the U.S.A.[7]

The striking rise in convention attendance pointed to a phenomenal growth in membership and numbers of chapters in the U.S. and around the world. At the 19th World Convention in San Francisco in 1972, it was reported that participation and attendance in the Fellowship had doubled in the previous two years, growing from 150,000 to 300,000 persons. These masses of people met in 900 chapters around the world, 700 of which were in the United States. In 1973, the reported statistics for all the activities of the Fellowship included 12,000 separate meetings, 3,500,000 in total attendance at all functions, publications (including magazines and books) reaching 29,500,000 readers, 100 T.V. stations with a possible viewership of 100,000,000 persons. The ultimate statistic was that of conversions. In that year 500,000 people were converted in ministries sponsored by the Fellowship. Overall, Shakarian estimated that 138,000,000 "lives had been touched" by the ministries of the Fellowship.[8]

The growth and size of the chapters was at times astounding. In Raleigh, N.C. interest was so high that organizers bought a bus and took about 40 men "from town to town" in a "Floating Prayer Meeting." The traveling chapter covered towns from Raleigh to Wilson, N.C. Across the country in Oklahoma City, the local chapter mushroomed under the leadership of local president Bill Mash until the officers were hard-pressed to find a restaurant large enough to hold the 1,500 who gathered for the monthly dinners.[9]

This indeed was a time of massive, uncontrolled growth for FGBMFI which in due course was bound to catch the attention of the public media. Around the nation stories began to appear in major newspapers and magazines detailing the size and scope of the Fellowship. On Sunday, July 16, 1972 the *New York Times* ran a major story titled, "Pentecostal Unit Gains Followers." This article gave *Times* readers around the world a positive summary of the ministry and explosive growth of the Fellowship. Another similar article in the *Jacksonville Florida Times-Union* in 1984 was titled, "Not A Church, But They've Found God." The author examined the lives and testimonies of such diverse members of the Jacksonville chapter as stockbroker Michael Darby, business executive Stephen J. De Sorbo, truck driver, Charles Moody, and surgeon, Dr.

Douglas Fowler, Jr.

By 1973, Shakarian reported that more than 4,000,000 persons had "met together to worship Jesus" in all the chapter meetings, conventions, and other activities of the Fellowship during the year. Also in 1974, he announced plans to found national headquarters in each country of the world with literature and radio broadcasts translated into 25 major languages. This program sent Fellowship men to the far corners of the world spreading the Full Gospel message. In October of 1976, a new chapter was organized in Jerusalem, a symbolic milestone for the organization. In addition chapters were later formed in such Islamic strongholds as Egypt and Saudi Arabia. Some of these chapters, which mainly served Western government, business, and military officials and their families, were the only Christian witness in those nations. New growth was especially rapid in Africa. In 1976, Shakarian reported that the Fellowship counted no less than 100 chapters in Africa. He was sure that "the Fellowship can now change the course of nations."[11]

The extraordinary growth of the Fellowship was also reflected in the finances received by the organization. In 1977, the officers published a full disclosure of the income that was received at the headquarters during the previous year. It included revenues of $4,020,088 and expenditures of $3,698,914 for a fund balance of $492,195. This money went to pay for the far-flung ministries of the Fellowship around the world. Although salaries were paid to an ever-growing office staff that handled the fast-growing affairs of the organization, not one cent of salary was paid to Shakarian or any of the other directors. Directors served as "a point of contact" to members all over the world. As Shakarian pointed out, they serve "without remuneration, pay their own expenses, and contribute generously to the support of this worldwide ministry."[12]

GOOD NEWS TELEVISION

Another sign of this rising tide of growth were the FGBMFI telecasts. They began in Los Angeles in 1965 with the telecast "Charismata in the 20th Century" and in 1970 with a local "talk show" sponsored by the Southern California chapters. In 1972 FGBMFI launched a national telecast called "Good News" sponsored around the nation by local chapters. Steve Shakarian, Demos' youngest son, came on board to head up Omega Advertising, the in-house agency that handled all the production and promotion. By 1973, the program was seen on 62 broadcast TV stations in the United States and 45 Canadian outlets. The schedules were run regularly in *Voice* for the benefit of members who promoted the program in their cities. At its zenith "Good News" was broadcast over 150 television and 70 radio stations throughout America. In addition to some of the newly established Christian networks such as Pat Robertson's Christian Broadcasting Network (CBN) and Jim Bakker's "Praise the Lord" (PTL) Network, "Good News" was the first nationally syndicated program that provided the listener with local phone numbers.[13]

Another TV ministry was the production of prime-time specials. "Good News America" was syndicated to the top 100 major American markets. A favorite technique was to edit the international conventions and show excerpts on the program. This was a telecast from the 1975 convention originating from Anaheim, California. It was co-hosted by Pat Boone and Demos Shakarian and featured Oral Roberts, Rex Humbard and Kathryn Kuhlman as special guests. This special won an Emmy award. The program provided telephone lines for viewer responses placed strategically throughout the nation. In some cities there were from 100 to 200 phones set up to receive calls. At its height, thousands of calls would come in from listeners. In Wilmington, N.C. 2,200 local calls came in after the airing of "The Happiest People" special in 1982. At one point over 150 letters arrived at the headquarters every working day from listeners all over the nation. In 1985 Pat Boone hosted the TV special "Turning Point." This dynamic media ministry led Shakarian to exclaim that with these telecasts "entire cities can be healed at one time."[14]

Some local chapters experienced incredible responses to the program. In Dayton, Ohio in 1977, the chapter president reported that "Good News TV has revolutionized this area." When a dinner for 500 was announced to support the program, 1,200 came, causing a logistical and culinary crises for the planners. To the delight of the planners, however, the banquet raised money for an entire year's support for the Dayton telecast.[15]

"At first we were reluctant about tongues being exhibited on the telecasts," said Mac Watson, president of Macon, Georgia FGBMFI chapter. But an early pilot featuring George Otis speaking in tongues passed the test of the CBS affiliate in Macon, Georgia where Shakarian was visiting. When Otis spoke in tongues, Watson reported "You could have heard a pin drop in the studio as all conversation ceased." It was "so natural and beautiful" that, with tongues and all, the station accepted the telecast. We couldn't afford the cost but the station gave us the time free.[16]

Another TV outreach of the Fellowship was the five-hour prime time telethon "Good News Tonight." The program featured live and taped interviews with people who had seen God's miracle-working power manifest in their lives. The finest in Gospel music, teaching segments by some of America's greatest Bible expositors, and a dynamic presentation of the Fellowship's six worldwide outreaches were also shown. Viewers were urged to phone in and request prayer for their needs and also to pledge donations. The top 16 markets were targeted. In the Cleveland/Akron market a powerful moving of God's Spirit was evident in both the studio and the viewer's homes. Telephone counselors answered more than 6,000 calls in Cleveland and Akron.[17]

The reports of lives changed by listening to the telecasts became the major motivation to support the television ministry, which by its very nature, was expensive to produce. A letter from an American businessman in Tokyo told of a man who "was about to go out into the night to commit an immoral act" when he heard "Good News" on the T.V. in his hotel room. The Gospel as proclaimed by fellow businessmen on the program caused him to stop, repent of his evil intentions, and turn his life over to Christ. "Thank you for saving my family," he wrote.[18]

A striking testimony in *Voice* told of an insurance salesman in Honolulu, Harold Shiraki, who had lost $20,000 to an "evil man" who with a judge had swindled him out of his life savings. Enraged, Shiraki bought a gun and made plans to kill them both. Before he could leave his house, however, he heard "Good News" on his T.V. and was overcome with remorse for his murderous plans. Falling on his knees, he repented and was converted. A former Buddhist, Shiraki was soon baptized in the Holy Spirit and became a flaming evangelist. His first prayer was for his sister who was so autistic that she could not even recognize any of her family. When his sister was instantly healed after Shiraki's prayer, his mother became an instant convert to

Christianity. After burning over 300 "gods" that she kept in her home, she called in her family and friends and over 300 of them were converted, one for every god that was burned. Later, Shiraki went back to Japan where more of his relatives were converted.[19]

With the advent of "low power" TV stations in the late 1970's, FGBMFI made ambitious plans to cover the nation with hundreds of inexpensive stations which could be built by local chapters. Other plans were made to build "thousands of translator" stations which could bring 24-hour Christian television to smaller towns and isolated rural areas of America untouched by the major networks. By 1981, the first translator was dedicated in Waterloo, Iowa by Shakarian who called for the Waterloo translator ministry to be "duplicated in hundreds of cities" in America. For a while it looked as if the low power and translator stations would grow into a major media ministry of the Fellowship. But the bright dreams for these projects never matched the success of the more traditional telecasts of "Good News" on the regular broadcast stations and on the Christian cable networks. In the end cable TV swept the market making low power stations economically unfeasible.[20]

CELEBRITIES ATTRACTED

Invited to speak on the "Good News" telecasts, as well as to the conventions and chapter meetings were many Christian and secular celebrities, most of whom were also featured in *Voice* articles. As the conventions got larger, an invitation to speak in a plenary session was a major achievement for many preachers as well as an opportunity for politicians to speak before large and influential crowds of well-to-do businessmen. Over the years several nationally known politicians mounted

FGBMFI platforms to address the faithful. These included George Wallace, Governor of Alabama, who in 1975 addressed the Birmingham chapter on "Old Fashioned Faith," and Julian Carroll, Governor of Kentucky who not only spoke on "The Fifty-Fourth Man," but testified to receiving the baptism in the Holy Spirit in a FGBMFI chapter in Frankfort, Kentucky.[21]

Another governor who was destined to become a two-term President, Ronald Reagan, once spoke to the Sacramento, California chapter on the subject of revival. Warming to his subject, he told the Full Gospelers that soon "we are going to see one of the great spiritual revivals of all time." When he ran for President in 1980, thousands of FGBMFI members supported his candidacy.[22] Other politicians featured in chapter meetings included Richard Nixon, James Watt, and Representative John Conlan.

At one time or another, Shakarian or other top FGBMFI officials met with Jimmy Hoffa, Fidel Castro, Francois Duvalier, and Ferdinand Marcos. On one occasion, a planned meeting with Nikita Krushchev was canceled at the last minute by the Chairman of the U.S.S.R. Meeting with these men, explained Shakarian, in no way implied approval of their politics or policies by the Fellowship, but was a sincere attempt to reach them with the Gospel. In every case, these meetings were unplanned and at times "miraculous opportunities" and represented to the Full Gospel Business Men an "open door" to witness for Christ.[23]

25TH ANNIVERSARY—ANAHEIM 1978

By the time the Fellowship celebrated its 25th anniversary in 1978, FGBMFI was engaged in a frenzy of projects and meetings around the world. In that year the Fellowship conducted 134 conventions, rallies, advances, and seminars. These were sponsored by

1,723 chapters in 66 nations. This period was also a high point for the television ministries sponsored by the Fellowship, with "Good News" outlets doubling in one year to 300 stations. In addition, the applications for translator stations reached a total of 425. Across the board, the membership and ministries of FGBMFI increased by 10% in one year.[24]

It was during these boom times for the Fellowship that Shakarian called on the members of FGBMFI to build a new headquarters building to handle the mushrooming work of administering the ever-growing empire. In the years since 1953, there had been six buildings in Los Angeles used for the headquarters staff, none of which were owned by the Fellowship except the building on Figueroa Street. Each one soon turned out to be too small for the staff of workers. By the middle of the 1970's it was estimated that the staff needed six times more space than was available. In May of 1975, while the Board was considering the problem of headquarters space, a prophecy through tongues and interpretation came forth:

> "You have spoken of a small seed being multiplied into a vast harvest. I say unto you this night, 'plant Me a seed and watch Me grow it. Watch Me water it and watch Me multiply it, and behold, you will see a miracle come forth before your eyes.'"[25]

Immediately a motion was made and unanimously passed to select a site and "initiate purchase plans" for a new headquarters to be located in Costa Mesa, California. Now was the time, said Shakarian to build a "World Laymen's Headquarters" that could serve the needs of the Fellowship for years to come. To raise funds for the project, the officers created a new base of donors known as the "Founder's Circle," members of which would give offerings for the project. Their

Their names would be inscribed in a "Founders' Circle Book" which would be prominently displayed inside the new building. Paul Toberty located the property and made his license available to begin the project. Soon architects and builders were busy designing the ultra-modern edifice on Bear Street which would contain 60,000 square feet of office space. The total cost was set at $3,000,000.[26]

While construction proceeded on the new headquarters building, plans were made for the 25th anniversary World Convention which was scheduled for July 3-8, 1978. No fewer than 25,000 persons attended this the "Silver Anniversary Celebration World Convention" in Anaheim, California. Speakers for this occasion included Paul Crouch, Maria Von Trapp, Pat Robertson, John Bertolucci, and of course, Oral Roberts. At this convention reports were given on the construction of the new international headquarters building in Costa Mesa, 25 miles from Shakarian's home in Downey. The on-sight construction manager for the project was Fred Rader, a retired GSA administrator who moved from Redding, California and spent eighteen months overseeing the building's construction. During this time, Rader worked without pay and gave witness to his faith to everyone who came near him. By the time the work was done, he claimed to have "witnessed to 200 passersby on the job, seeing five "saved" and one "baptized in the Holy Spirit."[27]

NEW HEADQUARTERS BUILDING—1980

The new headquarters building, the cost of which had ballooned from its original estimated cost of $3,000,000 to a total of $5,000,000 was finished and dedicated on January 27, 1980. Again, Oral Roberts on hand to give the keynote address. Serving as emcee was

Pat Boone who read greetings from President Jimmy Carter and Anwar Sadat, the President of Egypt. A gentle rain fell during the ceremonies which were held outside in front of the building. These, Oral Roberts proclaimed, were "God's tears of joy." Just before the ceremony ended, the sun made an "unusual appearance." This was seen as a good sign by those assembled.[28]

With Oral Roberts giving the main address, Shakarian and others remembered the little banquet in Clifton's Cafeteria in which Roberts had challenged the new Fellowship to plant 1,000 chapters in the world. By the time the new Headquarters building was dedicated, the Fellowship had long since surpassed that goal. As a matter of fact, by the end of the decade of the 1980's, FGBMFI numbered 2,646 chapters in the world, with 1,800 located in the United States alone. Every month, 600,000 to 700,000 people met in regular chapter meetings of the Fellowship, while it was estimated that all the evangelistic ministries of the group touched the lives of over one billion people.[29]

In many ways, the opening of the new ultramodern headquarters in Costa Mesa represented the high point in the history of the Fellowship. The worldwide growth and influence of FGBMFI had succeeded in making this by far the most successful and far-reaching laymen's organization in the history of Christianity. The Fellowship was now hitting the crest of the wave and standing on the heights with the rest of the American charismatic movement. In this period of giantism, FGBMFI participated in and played a leading role in other giant rallies sponsored by charismatics and Pentecostals.[30]

Just before the dedication of the headquarters in 1978, Full Gospel had participated in the massive 1977 Kansas City "General Ecumenical Conference on Charismatic Renewal in the Churches." Here over 50,000 charismatics of the "three streams" (Pentecostal, Protestant, and Catholic) met in Arrowhead Stadium to celebrate the outpouring of the Holy Spirit in the world. Probably most of those present had been touched by FGBMFI at one time or another.[31]

The Fellowship was also on hand to support the huge 1980 "Washington for Jesus" rally which filled the mall in the nation's capital with over 200,000 people demonstrating for a more Christian America. Planned to bring a Christian influence to bear in the presidential election of 1980, the mass rally was largely ignored by the press. The leader of the rally was John Gimenez, pastor of the "Rock Church" in Virginia Beach, Virginia, who had been a leading evangelist in the London FGBMFI "airlift" in 1965. Demos Shakarian was one of the major speakers at the mall. When later giant "Congresses on the Holy Spirit and World Evangelization" were held in New Orleans in 1987, and Indianapolis in 1990, FGBMFI breakfast sessions were held for standing-room only crowds.[32]

It is no coincidence that FGBMFI moved in influence and size with the charismatic renewal. To be sure, FGBMFI had played a major role in sparking the beginning and continuing growth of the movement both in America and in many other lands. In many ways, the life and course of FGBMFI was the best barometer of the growth and development of the renewal at large.

---

1. *The biographies of Coe, Branham and Hicks can be found in Burgess,* et.al., Dictoinary of Pentecostal and Charismatic Movements, *pp. 98, 222, and 390.*

2. *David Harrell in* Oral Roberts; An America Life, *has chronicled Robert's relationship with Shakarian and FGBMFI. See especially pp. 97, 153-155, 472-473.*

3. *Jerry Jensen, "Ecumenical Education," Voice, May 1967, pp. 8-13.*

4. Ibid., *pp. 8-10. For the complete story of the dedication see Harrell,* Oral Roberts; An American Life, *pp. 228-230.*

5. *See* Voice, *January 1961, p. 23.*

6. *Jerry Jensen, Personal interview with the author, February 15, 1992, Costa Mesa, California.*

7. *See* Voice, *October 1972, pp. 2-3 (San Francisco); November 1975, pp. 13-35 (Anaheim, 1975); July-August, 1977, pp. 30-37 (Washington); September 1978, pp. 18-24 (Anaheim, 1978). Also see May, 1979, p. 24 for the Phoenix Convention where room partitions had to be moved to make room for "overflow" crowds in the ballroom.*

8. *This data was given by Shakarian in, "Worldwide Outreach,"* Voice, *September 1974, pp. 17-24.*

9. *See "Floating Prayer Meeting,"* Voice, *September, 1972, p. 35. Bill Mash, personal interview with the author, Oklahoma City, May 16, 1992.*

10. *These figures were published in the* New York Times, *July 16, 1972. The* Times *article was re-printed in* Voice, *October, 1972, pp. 2-26. The* Florida Times-Union *article appeared on August, 18, 1984 and was republished in* Voice, *April, 1985, p. 22.*

11. *Shakarian, "Eight Memorable Days,"* Voice, *February, 1975, pp. 20-21. Also see February 1976, p. 15; and January, 1977, p. 10.*

12. *For the financial report see:* Voice, *July-August, 1978, pp. 17-20. Also see "International Directors,"* Voice, *March 1985, pp. 36-37.*

13. *For reports of the first television broadcasts, see "FGBMFI Goes to TV,"* Voice, *May, 1970, 36-37. Also see Zeigler, "Full Gospel," p. 322. Also see* Voice, *April 1973, pp. 22-23.*

14. *See "Good News America,"* Voice, *February, 1976, p. 16; and "Update,"* Voice, *April, 1975, p. 17. Also see Shakarian, "Look and Live,"* Voice, *June 27, 1977, p. 27. For the Wilmington story see "Update,"* Voice, *September, 1982, p. 24.*

15. *See* Voice, *July-August, 1977, p. 11.*

16. *For the story on Otis, see* Voice, *February, 1976, p. 35.*

17. *See* Voice, *April, 1976, p. 11.*

18. *Interview with Demos Shakarian, May 27, 1992.*

19. *Interview with Demos Shakarian, May 27, 1992. Also see, Harold Shiraki, "Good News,"* Voice, *February, 1973, pp. 19-21.*

20. *For promotion on the low power and translator TV stations see "Translators,"* Voice, *December, 1978, pp. 5-8; and "Signals From Space,"* September, 1981, pp. 2-7.*

21. *For the story of Governor Wallace, see* Voice, *May, 1976, p. 17; for Governor Carroll, April, 1984, pp. 2-6.*

22. *See* Voice, *April, 1970, p. 37.*

23. *For the Krushchev cancellation see* Voice, *October, 1959, pp. 9-10; for Hoffa October, 1961, pp. 1-4; for Marcos, October, 1984, p. 21.*

24. *The 1978 statistics are found in "FGBMFI Dateline,"* Voice, *January, 1979. p. 18.*

25. *See* Voice, *May 1976, p. 20; September 1976, p. 30.*

26. *See* Voice, *September, 1977, pp. 10-11.*

27. *See* Voice, *September, 1978, "World Convention and Silver Anniversary Celebration," 18-25. Fred Rader, "Yes,"* Voice, *February, 1980, pp. 26-29.*

28. *For photos of the gala dedication, see "The World Changers,"* Voice, *May 1980, pp. 3-17.*

29. *Shakarian, "The Fellowship in the '80's,"* Voice, *July 1982, pp. 6-7.*

30. *Jensen-Synan interview, February 15, 1992.*

31. *The flavor of the Kansas City Conference is given in David Manuel's,* Like a Mighty River, A Personal Account of the Charismatic Conference of 1977 *(Orleans, Massachusetts; Rock Harbor Press, 1977).*

32. *See "Washington For Jesus,"* Voice, *July-August, 1980, pp. 24-25. For more on the New Orleans and Indianapolis Congresses, see Vinson Synan and Ralph Rath,* Launching the Decade of Evangelization *(South Bend; North American Renewal Services Committee, 1990).*

Chapter Nine

THE MEN OF
THE FELLOWSHIP

*"These men may come from all walks of life and
from the various churches, but once a week they
become as one as they have their meal together, sing
hymns together, and give their testimony..."*
—Demos Shakarian

As Full Gospel Business Men's Fellowship International developed and matured, the very nature of the organization was to be seen in the men of the Fellowship. Although mostly made up of business and professional men, there were always thousands of men who were everyday farmers and laborers. All men who loved the Lord and who agreed with the faith and purposes of the Fellowship were welcomed to join and participate. The first generation of leaders were upscale Pentecostal businessmen, much like the founder, Demos Shakarian. They came from such churches as the Assemblies of God, the Pentecostal Holiness Church, the Church of God, the International Church of the Foursquare Gospel, and the Pentecostal Church of God. In general, they represented the upper level of Pentecostal laity, both economically and socially.

The first general officers of FGBMFI generally fit the foregoing description. Shakarian, himself, was the

model of what FGBMFI was all about. A third generation Pentecostal, he had risen to the middle class of California society and in most cases was dubbed "a
wealthy California dairyman." His was the story of a
family rising from Armenian immigrant poverty to
American prosperity. After selling his dairy in 1970, he
moved into real estate where he continued to prosper
as both a developer and buyer and seller of property.
Serving without salary from the beginning and making
generous financial contributions to FGBMFI, he served
as the prime model of what the Fellowship stood for, a
man who served God with all his heart, and in doing so
enjoyed an Old Testament type of prosperity which
closely paralleled his understanding of economics and
spirituality.

EARLY LEADERS

His first Vice-President, Lee Braxton, also served as
a shining example of what the Fellowship stood for.
Born in poverty in North Carolina, he was converted in
a small Pentecostal Holiness church in Whiteville, N.C.
Although he attended Holmes Bible College, in Greenville, S.C., he never felt called to preach. Through hard
work as a mechanic, he was able to rise to the place
where he could buy the automobile dealership where
he worked. He then founded a bank as well as several
other businesses in Whiteville.

In his early forties Braxton was ready to retire with
a secure future. Then he met Oral Roberts. Completely
captivated with the Oklahoma evangelist, he forgot
about retirement, moved his family to Tulsa, and spent
the rest of his life promoting the Roberts' radio and
television ministry. Although he was a solid businessman, Braxton was a talented spiritual and motivational
speaker who was in constant demand in local churches

and service clubs.[1]

Miner Arganbright was a constant challenge to Shakarian from the early days when he told Demos that he "wouldn't give a nickel for the whole outfit." But after the vision on the Oriental rug, he gave significant financial support which was indispensable to the early development of the Fellowship. Beginning as a masonry contractor, he rose to be a general contractor who built large commercial buildings in the Los Angeles area. An activist, Arganbright traveled around the world on behalf of the Fellowship and founded chapters wherever he went. His service to FGBMFI was so lengthy that at the age of 93 he was a featured speaker at the dedication of the new headquarters building in 1980, over a quarter century later. A long-time member of the Assemblies of God, Arganbright was a shining example of the first wave of classical Pentecostal leadership for FGBMFI.[2]

Another of the original officers, George Gardner, was a successful automobile salesman from Binghampton, New York who at one time led the New York zone in sales of General Motors automobiles, was a long-time leader in the Fellowship. Like Arganbright, Gardner was from the Assemblies of God and travelled as a lay evangelist and founded FGBMFI chapters as he went.[3]

The first Secretary-Treasurer of the Fellowship was Earl Draper, a certified public accountant from Fresno, California. A member of an Assemblies of God church in Fresno, Draper was a convert from the Church of Christ. He was present when the first slate of officers was elected in Fresno in 1952. Attending all of the initial meetings of the officers, he said of those days, "We didn't know exactly where we were going, but it was exciting just to know we were moving with God."

Draper was a voice of moderation in some of the early financial and leadership struggles of the Fellowship. He was a pivotal figure in 1955 when FGBMFI was over $10,000 in debt and was considering dropping the publication of *Voice* magazine. Through the influence of Draper and others, the third convention in Denver raised not only the $10,000 needed to continue *Voice,* but a grand total of $55,000 which guaranteed the continued ministry of the organization.[4]

Others who were prominent leaders in the Fellowship, although not national officers, included Michael Cardone (Assemblies of God) of Philadelphia, a "Master Rebuilder" of automobile parts, Erby Shaw (Pentecostal Holiness), of Greenville, S.C., a real estate developer, and Clifford Ford (International Church of the Foursquare Gospel) of Denver, a mass building contractor of new residences.[5]

Another early leader in the Fellowship was Jewel Rose of Shafter, California. Described as an "agriculturalist" he owned a huge farming ranch near Shafter which produced potatoes and other products. Converted in 1933 in a Pentecostal Church of God in Shafter, he had been one of the first men to join FGBMFI after its chartering in 1953. Elected as a Director of the Fellowship, Rose travelled extensively preaching and organizing FGBMFI chapters. In the three years from 1953 to 1956, he and his wife Florence traveled no less than 150,000 miles at his own expense ministering for the Fellowship. Jewel Rose gave generously to his church and to FGBMFI wherever he went. When an offering was given to pay his expenses, his usual response was to double the amount and give it to a local church or to the Fellowship. In 1955, he actually gave away more than he earned, explaining "You can't outgive God."[6]

A layman with a story similar to that of Rose, was Dr. Pierce P. Brooks of Dallas, Texas. A member and steward of the Tyler Street Methodist Church in Dallas,

Brooks had been active in helping his church build the largest Sunday school in American Methodism. His business credentials were impressive, serving as president of no less than five corporations and on the board of directors of many more companies. His major business activity was serving as founder and president of the National Bankers Life Insurance Company of Dallas where he conducted regular prayer meetings with his staff to pray about the problems with the company's business.

After joining FGBMFI, Brooks launched an evangelistic ministry that took him to many nations of the world. His meetings featured many claims to miraculous healings and of thousands being converted. Although he never held credentials as a licensed or ordained minister, Brooks was more successful than many full-time evangelists before his death in 1958. Unlike most of the earlier leaders of the Fellowship, Brooks was a member of a mainline Protestant church (Methodist) and not a classical Pentecostal. He was indeed a harbinger of things to come as more and more mainline churchmen were attracted to the Fellowship.[7]

An evangelist who in the 1960's led in the founding of many chapters in Texas, was the Rev. F.E. Ward, an Assemblies of God evangelist from Houston. By 1962 there was only one chapter in Texas, the one in Houston which Ward attended which had been founded by Andy Sorelle a few years before. In two years, Ward had established eight more chapters in Texas "with more in the making."

A man who commanded respect, Ward followed certain rules before he would organize a chapter. First, he would not begin with a "clique" or "split" in any city, and second, he would not start unless he had the "goodwill and at least the reasonable support of Full Gospel ministers." He was so successful that in the decade following 1962, he had founded over 100 chapters, mostly in Texas and Oklahoma. In time, Texas became one of the strongest states in the Fellowship, producing several national leaders. Also, many vital Hispanic chapters were organized in Texas as a result of Ward's vision.[8]

One of the most prolific organizers of chapters in America and overseas was Earl Prickett of Deptford, New Jersey. An "industrialist" who owned an industrial tank cleaning and pollution control service, Prickett was first attracted to the Philadelphia FGMBFI chapter simply because, as he said, "I went there planning to do business." His plans evaporated when the altar call was given. Coming forward, Prickett fell on his face, and "cried out desperately for God to have mercy on me and save me." Before arising, his white suit was covered with soot and "looked like a holstein cow, all black and white" according to Shakarian. He was also instantly delivered from alcohol, cigarettes, and healed of a kidney problem.[9]

From that point on Prickett, described as a "bundle of Holy Ghost energy," traveled all over the world in the interest of FGBMFI, founding chapters wherever he went. His most successful work was in the eastern states. As he traveled, he paid all his expenses out of his own pocket. In all, he founded over 100 chapters. To him, the Fellowship was "like a great multifaceted gem that sends out rays in every direction and to all people." When he died in 1990, Prickett was lauded as a "bright star" and "ardent supporter" of the Fellowship.[10]

A familiar face to thousands of Full Gospelers over the years was that of Al Malachuk, at one time president of the Washington, D.C. chapter. Of Russian descent, he and his brother Dan Malachuk, were raised in a Russian Pentecostal church in New York City. They both later affiliated with the Assemblies of God Church. While Dan went on to be a prominent publisher (*Logos* magazine), Al became founder of the huge Washington, D.C. regionals and "toastmaster" for many FGBMFI world and regional conventions. Always recognizable by his bald head and bow tie, Malachuk added a touch of humor to the many banquets and conventions that he helped to organize and emcee. He was lovingly called "Our Man in Washington" by the leadership of the Fellowship. His business was described as that of "manufacturer's representative."[11]

Two lawyers from Atlanta, Lynwood Maddox and Kermit Bradford, made significant contributions to the Fellowship over the years. While Maddox was a practicing attorney, Bradford became a judge of the Civil Court of Fulton County, Georgia. Bradford spoke of himself as a "licensed Methodist layman."[12]

LATER LEADERS

Three men who later played significant roles in the leadership of FGBMFI rose to prominence during the 1960's were Thomas Ashcraft, Norman Norwood, and Gene M. Ellerbee. An early leader in the movement, Ashcraft had been instrumental in founding the Atlanta chapter in 1955, the chapter that produced Maddox and Bradford.[13]

In time, the Atlanta chapter became one of the largest in the nation. Ashcraft was born in Arkansas, but made a business success as a baking company executive in Houston, Texas. After joining FGBMFI, he rose to be a Vice-President of the Fellowship and soon had the complete confidence of Shakarian, so much so that in 1982 the president tapped him for the newly-created position of "Executive Vice-President." At the dedication of the new headquarters in Costa Mesa in 1980, and from then on, Ashcraft was at Shakarian's side helping to direct the affairs of the Fellowship.[14]

Another Texan, Norman Norwood, was a home builder and real estate developer in Houston. Norwood had been converted in a Baptist church, but became a "Pentecostal Baptist" after receiving the baptism in the Holy Spirit under the ministry of John Osteen. After joining the Houston chapter of FGBMFI, he rose rapidly in the organization, rising to the position of International Director. In time he was to become a chief rival of Shakarian and temporarily succeeded in removing him from power.[15]

Gene M. Ellerbee, who also was to play an important leadership role in the Fellowship, came to prominence in the business world as the worldwide sales manager for Procter and Gamble, one of the largest corporations in America. Born in San Antonio, Texas, he eventually moved to the corporate headquarters in Cincinnati after successful stints as regional sales manager in Virginia, Nebraska, Florida and California. Although born a Catholic, Ellerbee for a time became an agnostic after the untimely death of his daughter. In 1978, however, he was converted to Christ through the witness of his wife and several Christian friends. Afterwards he became active in the Cincinnati chapter of Full Gospel Business Men, leading a successful prison ministry where hundreds of prisoners were converted and baptized in the Holy Spirit.[16]

BUSINESS MEN, LARGE AND SMALL

In the early days of the Fellowship's history, a book appeared entitled *God's Formula for Success and Prosperity,* edited by Oral Roberts and G.H Montgomery. Most of the men featured in the book were associated with FGBMFI and as such served as a guide to the type of men promoted by the Fellowship. Each chapter of the book was a short biography of a businessman who had done well. They were: Clifford Ford, "God's Real Estate Man," (7-20); Henry Krause, "God's Plowman," (21-38), Demos Shakarian, "God's Dairyman," (39-54); Nick Timko, "God's Tool and Die Maker," (55-64); George Gardner, "God's Automobile Man," (65-74); Ralph Quest, "God's Contractor," (75-84); Jack Linn, "God's Poultryman," (85-104); Albert Ott, "God's Ministering Servant," (105-118); Lee Braxton, "God's Banker," (119-136); Solomon John Mattar, "God's Keeper of the Tomb," (137-146); and Oral Roberts "God's Man for this Hour," (147-158).[17]

Most of these were self-made men who had risen from poverty and obscurity to a comfortable status of wealth and prosperity. But they were not representatives of the top echelon of America's business elite. Although some, like Shakarian, came from large cities such as Los Angeles, many more were from small-town America, i.e. Whiteville, North Carolina (Braxton), Binghampton, New York (George Gardner), and Hutchinson, Kansas (Henry Krause). According to Robert Mapes Anderson, most of the early Full Gospel Business Men were lower middle class, white collar employees mixed with some laborers. Businessmen were probably in the minority, at least at the outset of the movement. Although some were wealthy, most were not. But they all shared the dream that they or anyone else could prosper if they followed the Lord in the fullness of the Holy Spirit.[18]

Some observers feel that association with FGBMFI was often a positive financial benefit to the members of the Fellowship, and that many came to Fellowship meetings for material rather than spiritual motives. In Anderson's view, for many men, the contacts made in chapter meetings could be "highly profitable." Not only did the members receive positive messages about faith and prosperity, they were often able to make important business connections with their fellow worshippers.

The "positive confession" prosperity message which was proclaimed in FGBMFI chapters and conventions by such speakers as Kenneth Hagin and Kenneth Copeland, linked financial success with spiritual fervor and power. In a classic testimony from a Virginia chapter, a member said:

> "Before the baptism in the Holy Spirit, I was climbing the ladder of success, jealous of those ahead of me. Now I realize that my strength comes from God and He looks out for me. Success comes easier for me and without walking over others. I am also more free to share my faith with others as my personal reputation is no longer my primary concern." [19]

The success ethos of the Fellowship was appealing not only to small businessmen on the way up, but eventually to those who already had reached the pinnacle of business success. Although the founders had mostly consisted of rising businessmen in small towns working their way up from poverty, the leaders who came on board in the 1980's included some executives who had already made the Fortune 500 list of American corporate business giants.

1985 ORGANIZATIONAL ASSESSMENT

This 1985 organizational assessment of FGBMFI done by Steve Shakarian, who became Chief Operating Officer in 1980, shed light on the types of men who belonged to the Fellowship at that time. The mean age for presidents was 48 years, indicating that the Fellowship was aging, at least in leadership. The vast majority of presidents were caucasian (92%), married (95%), well-educated (43% had finished four years of college, 30% had graduated, while another 38% had attended some college), business employees (while 32% owned their own businesses, 56% were "employees of some company"). The most common occupational fields were "services, professions, and manufacturing."[20]

Rather than being an organization of the rich, FGBMFI chapter presidents were usually men of modest means. For instance, in 1985 the average annual household income was reported to be $28,500. The income for the average member, $27,500, was only slightly lower than that of presidents. Although the chapters were almost evenly divided between rural, urban, and suburban areas, the greatest growth in membership was experienced in suburban locations.[21]

The size of the businesses represented in the Fellowship in 1985 tended to be on the smaller side of the ledger. The survey showed the following profile for the annual revenues of the businesses owned by the officers:

> Less than $100,000 . . . . 8%
> $100,000 to $1 million 11%
> $1 million to $50 million 14%
> Over $50 million 7%
> Don't know/no answer 60%

Nevertheless, the small number of officers of large corporations became a more important group as time went by. A key executive interview series in *Voice* which was conducted by Steve Shakarian and Jerry Jensen in 1986 and 1987 featuring corporate Chief Executive Officers (CEO's) indicated how the scope of FGBMFI had risen since the 1950's. *Voice* now featured top executives of some of the nation's largest corporations. Included in the list were Allen Mayer of Oscar Mayer meat packing fame; Sam Moore, CEO of Thomas

Nelson Publishers; Jim Buick of Zondervan Publishers; John DeLorean of DeLorean Motors, Inc.; Chuck Buck of Buck Knives; Sanford McDonnell of the McDonnell-Douglas aircraft manufacturing company; Peter Grace, Chairman of W.R. Grace Company; and Gene M. Ellerbee, worldwide manager of sales operation of Procter & Gamble. In other issues before and after this series, articles were published featuring Lee Buck of New York Life Insurance Company, and Jack Eckerd of Eckerd's Drug Store chain. A different type of CEO also featured was General Ralph Haines, at one time commanding general of the U.S. Continental Army Command.[22]

This list of Full Gospel Business Men demonstrated the social and denominational roots of this newer generation of leadership. In contrast to the first wave of leaders who came mostly from classical Pentecostal churches, these businessmen were usually from charismatic movements in the mainline Protestant and Catholic churches. For example, Buck and Haines were Episcopalians, Eckerd a Presbyterian, and Grace a Roman Catholic. The few classical Pentecostals who made it on this level were mostly recent converts to Pentecostalism from mainline churches. Another difference was that many of these CEO's were from that citadel of American capitalism, New York City.

PROFESSIONAL MEN

Despite the words "Business Men" in its name, the Fellowship accepted any man who desired to belong as long as he accepted the beliefs and practices of the organization. This applied especially to members of the professions who were highly welcomed and spotlighted in the meetings and publications of FGBMFI. Lawyers, medical doctors, and educators were especially welcomed in Full Gospel circles from the earliest days.

In fact, the first series of booklets published by the Fellowship featured the relationship of members of the various professions to the baptism in the Holy Spirit. The initial issue entitled *Attorney's Evidence on the Baptism in the Holy Spirit* appeared in 1965. This was followed in 1967 by another entitled *Physicians Examine the Baptism in the Holy Spirit.* The military profession was covered in a 1969 book which appeared during the height of the Vietnamese war entitled *Voices of the Military.*

The field of medicine was covered in the 1972 volume entitled *A Sure Cure: Acts of the Holy Spirit Within the Medical Profession Today.* Attorneys were given a second look in *God and the Lawman* which also appeared in 1972. Professional educators were covered in the last of the series entitled *The Scholarship of the Spirit: The Acts of the Holy Spirit Among Educators Today* which appeared in 1977.

The common thread in all these booklets was that, whatever a man's profession might be, the experience of the baptism in the Holy Spirit with the evidence of speaking in tongues added a surefire boost toward success in the field. The book, *A Sure Cure,* included testimonies of no less than 14 medical doctors who not only administered medicine and surgery, but also prayer to their patients. These testimonies, as well as the others, were read avidly by members of the various professions and were often given as gifts by members who desired to invite professional friends to local chapter meetings. They were effective recruiting tools indeed.

MILITARY MEN

Over the years, the American military was high-lighted in chapter meetings, banquets, special convention dinners, and in special military issues of *Voice* magazine. Although the policy of the Fellowship was to avoid partisan politics, the basic conservative stance of most of the members was apparent in the publications of the organization. It is John Mapes Anderson's contention that FGBMFI was "petit-bourgeois," "anti-communist," "pro-capitalist," "anti-socialist" and in favor of the American free enterprise system. This conclusion should not be surprising since the Fellowship was essentially a society of Spirit-filled capitalists trying to make good in the business world.[23]

It could well be said that FGBMFI was essentially a politically conservative group. One study found that only 3% of most members described themselves as "liberal." Given the political orientation of most members, it would probably be accurate to say that the Fellowship thought of itself as part of the "Christian Right" during the years following World War II, and that most FGBMFI members allied themselves with the military in the Korean conflict of the 1950's and the Vietnamese war of the 1960's and 1970's.

Some of the military figures promoted on the pages of *Voice* and in speaking engagements included James E. Johnson, Assistant Secretary of the Navy, and General Ralph Haines, the Four Star Commanding General of the U.S. Continental Army Command. Johnson, a black man, was one of the first Afro-Americans to gain prominence in the Fellowship. Long after leaving his post with the Navy, Johnson continued to be in demand as a speaker in Full Gospel rallies and dinners.[24]

General Haines became the star attraction at several military banquets that were held at national conventions during the Vietnam war era. His testimony was that after being "born again" he received the baptism in the Holy Spirit at a FGBMFI retreat in Buffalo, N.Y. in 1971. Thereafter, Haines, an Episcopalian, was a tireless preacher and teacher on the Full Gospel circuit, and an often used figure in the military breakfasts that were sometimes featured in local, regional, and national conventions.

THE HEALING EVANGELISTS

The group of men who helped the Fellowship most in its formative years were the evangelists who gave visibility and spiritual direction to the Fellowship. Although they were constitutionally barred from holding full membership in the Fellowship, their influence was crucial to the success of FGBMFI. Their contributions were all the more important since the pastors and leaders of most Pentecostal denominations largely ignored or at times actively opposed the ministry of the Fellowship. In some ways, the rise of FGBMFI could be seen as a protest movement against the laid-back policy of the major Pentecostal churches toward the healing evangelists. One could say that the relationship between the evangelists and the Fellowship was a symbiotic one, especially in the early years.

As a possible reaction to the rise of FGBMFI, some of the Pentecostal denominations organized their own men's fellowship organizations. This was of great concern to Shakarian and the officers of Full Gospel Business Men's Fellowship, mainly due to the small circulation of *Voice* in the early days. Since FGBMFI strongly supported the healing evangelists, some of them soon began to publicize the annual conventions of the Fellowship in their magazines, sometimes with full page ads offered at no cost. This cooperation was vital to the development of the Fellowship in its formative stages.[26]

The one evangelist who played a consistent role during the entire history of the Fellowship was Oral Roberts. From the very first chapter meeting at Clifton's Cafeteria in 1951 to the dedication of the new headquarters in 1980, to the annual convention in 1991, Roberts was a constant supporter of Shakarian and his vision of a world layman's revival. It was Roberts who counseled Shakarian to abandon the large convention centers and return to the ballrooms where FGMBFI members could sit down at the "banqueting table" and be "Ballroom Saints" again in 1991. As the Fellowship approached its fortieth anniversary celebration in 1992, Roberts and Shakarian were in their familiar position as first evangelist and first layman of the organization.

Over the years other evangelists made important contributions to the growth of the Fellowship, among them Tommy Hicks, William Branham, and Jack Coe, but it was Roberts who towered over them all. An early controversy concerned the latter years of the ministry of William Branham. Although he saw FGBMFI as his "denomination," Branham encountered opposition from such respected neo-Pentecostal leaders as Harald Bredesen and James Brown. From the beginning until Branham's untimely death in 1965, Shakarian fully supported his ministry within the Fellowship. His death ended the possibility of serious problems within the organization that had brought him to worldwide prominence.[27]

By 1992, it was difficult to see any other evangelists on the horizon who could duplicate the roles played by Roberts, Hicks, and Branham in the life of the Fellowship. The newer generation of healing evangelists, such as Reinhard Bonnke in Germany and Carlos Anacondia in Argentina were not in a position to influence the Fellowship as had the first wave of healing evangelists.

THE TEACHERS

Ranking just behind the evangelists in ministerial influence were the teachers who were brought in to teach the afternoon crowds who flocked to FGBMFI conventions. Among these were Derek Prince, Bob Mumford, Charles Simpson, and Don Basham, sometimes known as the "Fort Lauderdale Four." In the early 1970's these men were in high demand, not only in FGBMFI circles, but in the burgeoning charismatic renewal conferences to explain the baptism in the Holy Spirit, divine healing, the casting out of demons and other aspects of Pentecostal spirituality to masses of people hungry for a fresh presentation of biblical teaching on these subjects.

In a short time, these men developed a system of teaching which they called "discipleship" and "shepherding" which they hoped would bring some order to the billowing waves of charismatics who came to hear them teach. By the mid-1970's these teachers had aligned themselves with such growing Catholic charismatic communities as the Word of God in Ann Arbor, Michigan and the People of Praise in South Bend, Indiana. Their teaching concerning spiritual authority became extremely controversial, especially in FGBMFI and among such televangelists as Pat Robertson.

The upshot of the controversy came in 1975 when FGBMFI and Robertson's 700 Club forbade the appearance of any of the Fort Lauderdale teachers in any chapters, conventions, or T.V. broadcasts. After being banned from Full Gospel and television, the shepherding movement rapidly disintegrated and by 1990 had practically disappeared from the charismatic scene.

Another controversial group of teachers that managed to retain the support of FGBMFI were the "Faith" teachers, led by Kenneth Hagin and Kenneth Copeland. These men first rose to prominence in the early 1970's largely through their ministry in Full Gospel chapters. Hagin was an unknown Southern Pentecostal evangelist until he began to receive invitations to lead "Holy Ghost" seminars in FGBMFI conventions across the nation. His teaching booklets sparked a burgeoning ministry which eventually led to the founding of the Rhema Bible Institute in Broken Arrow, Oklahoma in 1974.[28]

Kenneth Copeland, who had his first ministerial experience as a student at Oral Roberts University in the 1960's, became a prominent teacher at FGBMFI conventions in the same manner as Hagin, as a "Holy Ghost" teacher in afternoon workshops. In a short time, however, Copeland's ministry began to skyrocket largely due to the exposure he received in FGBMFI circles.[29]

The ministry of Hagin and Copeland centered around the teaching of "positive confession" for healing and prosperity, a movement that some critics lampooned as the "name it and claim it" gospel. Although the teachings of Hagin and Copeland stirred storms of theological controversy including several hostile books, the storm never seems to have touched FGBMFI. As of 1990, the faith teachers continued to be in the good graces of the Fellowship and welcome speakers at major conventions. Although the faith teachers generated much controversy within the Pentecostal churches and the charismatic renewal leadership, they retained a loyal following on the Full Gospel speaking circuit.

These were the men of the Fellowship: the leaders,

the businessmen, the evangelists, the teachers, and many others too numerous to mention. These were the men who made Full Gospel Business Men a mighty force in the earth. Led by Shakarian and his unshakable vision, they planted the banners of FGBMFI to the far corners of the earth. Despite all their shortcomings and the criticisms of their enemies, Full Gospel Business Men succeeded in sowing seeds of Pentecostal blessing and prosperity around the world in a way no other organization could possibly have done.

1. The major study of Braxton's life is a J. Larry Riley thesis entitled, "J. Lee Braxton—Mr. Layman" (Unpublished manuscript, Oral Roberts University, 1991). ORU houses Braxton's extensive papers. Braxton was an often featured writer in Voice *and speaker in FGBMFI conventions. His philosophy and accomplishments can be found in* Voice, *April, 1956, p. 23; "A Better Way," April 1972, pp. 4-30; "The Braxton Story," August 1983, p. 35. His obituary was run in* Voice, *July/August, 1983, pp. 32-38.*

2. See "Religion in Business Brings Sure Success," Voice, *February, 1953, pp. 8-11. See "Portals of Faith,"* Voice, *January, 1980, pp. 2-21. Also see Demos Shakarian's obiturary of Arganbright entitled, "The Man Who Changed His Mind," in* Voice, *June, 1987, p. 12.*

3. See "George Gardner Leads in Auto Sales," Voice, *February-March, 1955, p. 14. Also see Roberts and Montgomery,* God's Formula for Success and Prosperity, *pp. 65-74.*

4. See Earl Draper, "We Didn't Know Exactly Where we Were Going...But We Knew We Were Moving With God," Voice, *May 1978, pp. 20-24.*

5. See Michael Cardone, "The Master Rebuilder," Voice, *June 1977, pp. 22-24; W. E. Shaw, "Purposeful Prosperity,"* Voice, *June, 1977, pp. 2-32. The many articles by or about Ford include* Voice, *March 1956, p. 16; January, 1961, pp. 28-29. His obituary appeared in March, 1986, p. 22.*

6. See "The Conversion of Jewel Rose," Voice, *April, 1956, pp. 3-12.*

7. For Voice *articles on Brooks see: Pierce Brooks, "God is My Parner," October 1954, pp. 4-7; "Dr. Pierce Brooks' Jamaica Campaign," May 1956, pp. 4-9; and "Pierce Brooks is God's Partner Now," July 1958, pp. 3-9.*

8. See "Rev. F.E. Ward is...Paving a Path of Progress," Voice, September, 1963, p. 25.

9. See "Earl Prickett Appointed as Field Representative," Voice, March, 1960, p. 23.

10. "Earl Prickett—Industrialist," Voice, July, 1984, pp. 26-28; "Earl Prickett Remembered," Voice, October, 1990, p. 9. Interview with Demos Shakarian, May 17, 1992.

11. See "Al Malachuk," Voice, October 1963, p. 22; and "Our Man in Washington," Voice, September, 1969, pp. 4-33.

12. Lynwood Maddox, "The Perfect Partnership," Voice, May 1964, pp. 22-25. Kermit Bradford, "God Answered My Methodist Mother's Prayers," Voice, July-August, 1963, pp. 12-13; "The Judge's Decision," Voice, September 1970, pp. 4-28.

13. Tom Ashcraft, "Chapter is Planned for Atlanta," Voice, December 1955, p. 24.

14. A cover story on Ashcraft in Voice clearly conveyed Ashcraft's prominence at the time. See Thomas Ashcraft, "Called to Share," Voice, June, 1986, pp. 1-11.

15. See Norman Norwood, "The Lift of Love," Voice, April, 1975, pp. 2-9.

16. Gene M. Ellerbee, "A Thirst For Power," Voice, January, 1987, pp. 2-11.

17. Oral Roberts and G. H. Montgomery, eds., God's Formula For Success and Prosperity (Tulsa; America's Healing Magazine, 1955).

18. Robert Mapes Anderson, Personal Interview with the author. Lakeland, Florida, November 8, 1991.

19. See Bradfield, Neo-Pentecostalism; A Sociological Assessment, p. 45.

20. Steve Shakarian, "Organizational Assessment of Full Gospel Business Men's Fellowship International," April, 1985, pp. 24-25.

21. Ibid.

22. The CEO series appeared in several issues of Voice in 1986. They were as follows: Allen Mayer, February, 1986; Sam Moore, March, 1986; John DeLorean, April, 1986; Chuck Buck, May, 1986; Sanford McConnell, August, 1986. The Eckard story appeared in Voice, November, 1987; the Ralph Haines testimony appeared in January, 1972; the Jim Buick story in July, 1987; while the Peter Grace story appeared in March, 1987.

Lee Buck, who later became an important leader in FGBMFI, was featured in several issues of Voice. See November, 1974, p. 20 for his testimony. Also see "Assured Insurance," June, 1975, pp. 2-8; and "Is Life Insurance Enough," August, 1984, pp. 2-7. Gene M. Ellerbee was featured in January, 1987, pp. 2-11.

23. Personal interview with author at the Society for Pentecostal Studies, November, 1991.

24. See James E. Johnson, "A Lesson I'll Never Forget," Voice, July/August, 1973, pp. 20-21.

25. Ralph E. Haines, Jr., "Christian Renewal," and "How Deeply Moved Was I," Voice, January, 1972, pp. 13-19.

26. Interview with Demos Shakarian, May 27, 1992.

27. See Shakarian, "In Memorium," Voice, January-February, 1966. In this article announcing the sudden death of Branham it was said that "Branham often stated that the only fellowship to which he belonged was FGBMFI."

28. See Vinson Synan, "The Faith of Kenneth Hagin," in Charisma Magazine, *June, 1990, pp. 63-70.*

29. See Kenneth Copeland, "Update: Blackpool Convention: Copeland in Participating Ministry," Voice, November, 1983, pp. 22-23.

Chapter Ten

THE TESTIMONIES

"FGBMFI is like a great multifaceted gem that sends out rays in every direction and to all people. Daily and hourly, it is fulfilling the Bible prophecy of the great day of the laymen's revival."
—*Earl Prickett*

Among the many ingredients that caused FGBMFI to grow was the central place given in chapter meetings and on the pages of *Voice* to simple testimonies of everyday men and women overcoming everyday problems. To be sure, the Fellowship enjoyed able and prophetic leadership and good organization, but the fuel that fired the movement was the regular flood of testimonies of people from all walks of life, both rich and poor, who found help at the meetings.

The testimonies came in all sizes, shapes and forms, but most of them followed a common pattern that generally held true over the years. A typical testimony was that of Tom Battle of Kingwood, Texas who spoke of early poverty, early business success ("I became a multi-millionaire at 32 years old") a relapse into a sinful lifestyle (alcohol, marijuana, cocaine, pornography, adultery) maintenance of outside appearances, nominally religious, economic problems, a health crisis (wife suffered a heart attack), healing, (wife and child miracu-

lously healed), a crisis conversion to Christ (in despera-
tion while contemplating suicide), and baptism in the
Holy Spirit with tongues as evidence (usually at an
FGBMFI meeting). Most testimonies as published in
Voice had most, if not all, of the foregoing elements in
common.[1]

SINS OF THE FLESH

Many testimonies told of deliverance from the
many sins of the flesh and spirit that plague society at
large, but which seldom were cured in regular church
services. Many were the stories of victory over drugs,
adultery, homosexuality, alcoholism, pornography and
gambling. Others told of victory over rock and roll
music, rage against wives and children, and a rejection
of organized religion. Many told of lives wrecked in the
Korean and Vietnam wars, and subsequent deliverance
through the ministry of dedicated laymen from
FGBMFI who cared enough to tell them about Jesus.

A wrenching tale of addiction and deliverance was
given by George Morrison of Arvada, Colorado who
told of being an alcoholic as a boy followed by LSD
addiction in the Air Force: "After my first hit we
howled at the moon for three hours." Most of the time
he and his friends were constantly high on drugs. "We
would mix opium, marijuana and LSD in our beer,
guzzle it down and lay on the runway underneath landing aircraft." After the war, he was converted in an
FGBMFI meeting in Denver, Colorado where he came
under the impression that "all Christians in the world
lived in Denver." Another story of freedom from drugs
was from a drug dealer, Jim Janz who was busted in
Canada for selling marijuana. While in prison in Van-
couver, B.C. he was given copies of *Voice* and the
Bible. After reading both, he was converted, became a

jail trustee, and was ultimately freed.[2]

Another more middle class addiction, workaholism, was described in a testimony from Jim McEwan in his "Confessions of a Workaholic." Although he "loudly proclaimed Christ first, wife second, children third, job last," he found himself putting his "work first and valium second" in a vain attempt to succeed in the business world. The baptism in the Holy Spirit set him free from both valium and workaholism.[3] Other middle-class addictions, gambling and alcohol, plagued Bill Freeman of Statesboro, Georgia, who after his conversion was healed of cirrhosis of the liver and went on to be a minister of the Gospel. After his deliverance, Freeman the former "Ramblin Gamblin" man, used his testimony to get other men converted.[4]

Many were the testimonies of deliverance from sexual addictions and perversions, all instantly cured by the baptism in the Holy Spirit. At least two testimonies were published by former homosexuals who were healed and later lived normal lives. One, Ron Jesser of Cave Junction, Oregon, was later married and fathered two daughters. Another, Jim Johnson of Long Beach, California lived a double life with several lovers before being delivered through the ministry of "Homosexuals Anonymous." Others found deliverance from transexuality ("Trapped in the Wrong Body"), and pornographic addiction ("I Led Three Lives"), and male menopause ("A Man in Mid-Life Crisis").[5]

Probably the most common addiction confronted by the FGBMFI membership over the years was that of tobacco. Although the rules did not forbid smokers from attending or even belonging to the Fellowship, there was an unwritten understanding that smoking was an evil that needed to be exorcised from a Christian's life. From Pentecostalism there was a feeling that the Holy Spirit and nicotine could not dwell in the same temple at the same time. In FGBMFI meetings, peer pressure was against all addictions, especially alcohol and tobacco. Many chapter meetings ended with packs of cigarettes on the floor, thrown away by the newly-freed ex-smoker.

Among the testimonies of deliverance from the evil weed was that of Jim Ripley, a heavy smoker for 17 years. After being born again in a local church, he began to hunger for the baptism in the Holy Spirit, but felt that he could never give up his cigarettes. One night while driving home from church, he said "As I got into my car to go home, I reached for my cigarettes and lit one up. All of a sudden I had a sore throat." After praying for deliverance, he was baptized in the Holy Spirit and sang in tongues, and at the same time was freed from his tobacco addiction. "Since that night," he said, "I have never once had the slightest urge for a cigarette."[6]

THE ATHLETES

Over the years, many testimonies were published in *Voice* about leading athletes from many fields of sports. At times special sports issues were published filled with such testimonies. A favorite Christian sports figure was Tom Landry, the long-time coach of the Dallas Cowboys football team. In an article entitled "Winning; Is It Most Important?," Landry said that his teams never prayed for victory but "we pray to thank God for what He has given us—the opportunity to play. We pray to be the best that we can be and for protection from injury." In a similar vein, Jim Ryun, once the "fastest man alive," said in 1983 that "No, I'm not the fastest man alive anymore. I don't need to be. Running with Jesus has brought me the freedom and happiness that running for myself never could."[7]

Almost every sport imaginable was covered at one time or another with testimonies of spiritual victory if not always victory on the field. Kyle Rote, one of the first American soccer heroes who played for the New York Giants and the Houston Hurricanes, won the "Superstar" award in 1974. To him, however, Jesus Christ was the true superstar of all time. Other lesser known sports figures covered on the pages of *Voice* were; Robert Birdsong, "Mr. Universe" of 1974; William Besmanoff, a German Olympic boxer; David Story, "The Arm Wrestler;" Gene Burress who, like many other Americans said that "golf was my god" until he was converted; and Ed Dmitri who suffered from "Black Belt Obsession" until he was saved and baptized in the Holy Spirit.[8]

Some sports testimonies included miraculous healings that led to Christian ministry. Perhaps the most striking one was the story of Harold Cole, the 1983 champion water skier from Asheboro, North Carolina who broke his neck in a trampoline accident in 1984. Fearing that he would be a quadriplegic for life, he cried out to the Lord and was instantly healed. He then devoted the rest of his life to being an evangelist for the Assemblies of God.[9]

It was in the area of sports that African-Americans appeared most often on the pages of *Voice* as well as in FGBMFI chapter meetings. In 1987, Mychal Thompson of the Los Angeles Lakers admitted that he wanted to be "the first black Joe Namath," but his 6'9" height made that impossible. A committed Christian, he confessed that to him, "Jesus is my main hero," followed closely by Julius Erving, Charles Barkley, and Ralph Sampson.[10]

Perhaps the most popular black athlete to speak on the Full Gospel circuit was Meadowlark Lemon, the "Clown Prince" of the Harlem Globetrotters. Converted while still in his prime as a basketball player, he toured the world with fellow Christians Rosie Greer and Elgin Baylor attempting to win young people from a life of sin. He was greatly influenced by a T.V. minister, Fred Price, who later became his pastor.[11]

Another world famous black athlete featured by the Fellowship was Carl Lewis, the Olympic champion who won four gold medals for the United States in the 1984 Olympics. Born again in 1981 at an NCAA track and field championship meet in Baton Rouge, Louisiana, Lewis stood out as a runner who refused to use steroids and yet went on to beat the best runners in the world. In speaking of the 1988 Olympic games, he told his *Voice* readers:

> In the 1988 Olympics "I will be running not only for myself and my country, but for my Lord and Saviour Jesus Christ."[12]

AIRPLANE TESTIMONIES

Probably no topic was more often the subject of testimonies than those that concerned airplane disasters or near disasters. Perhaps this was due to the fact that businessmen were forced to travel so much by air that fear of flying lurked under the surface of many of their minds. At least two officers of the Fellowship, Lee Braxton and C.C. Ford, experienced plane crashes from which each narrowly escaped death. Ford was especially famous for his testimony of flying 200 miles on an empty tank of gas. Several others claimed similar experiences.

The most incredible survivor's testimony was that of Norman Williams who was in the worst air accident in history, at Tenerife in 1979. In this crash 593 persons died and only 60, including Williams, survived. He reported to *Voice* readers that as flames engulfed him, he began to quote Isaiah 43:1-2, "When thou walkest through the fire, thou shalt not be burned; neither shall the flame kindle upon thee." As he walked unscathed through the flames to safety, he kept repeating aloud, "I stand upon Your Word. I stand upon Your Word."[13]

Others claimed equally miraculous escapes. Frank Foglio, an early FGBMFI leader, was on a plane about to land in Spokane, Washington when the pilot announced an emergency landing due to a stuck landing gear. As he prayed, Foglio said "I clearly saw three angels underneath the plane, flitting back and forth like hummingbirds between the two wings and the landing gears." The plane eventfully came down on foam to a "perfect" landing, "three angels had guided it in all the way" said Foglio. Another case was involved the crash of a Stearman acrobatic plane in 1982, piloted by Bill Stinson. According to Stinson, the plane suddenly stalled and crashed to the ground, "spun over the top, dug a trench 4 feet deep," and then "tumbled over." Miraculously he and a friend walked away "without a scratch."[14]

In one of the most incredible testimonies ever, Jerry Wilkins told of flying a spraying plane from Idaho to Maine when "all the instruments failed" including the radio. Later the engine sprang an oil leak in addition to the failure of the manifold pressure gauge and the temperature gauges. In his desperation Wilkins yelled "Jesus, You gotta help me." Miraculously he landed safely. Perhaps the man who was saved the most was Charles Carney of Kansas City, Missouri. During his career in Vietnam and as an airline pilot for Braniff Airlines he survived: a parachute that failed to open (it later did open), the crash of a gunship, an airliner that lost a tire, and an engine that caught on fire.

Not all pilots had horror stories of crashes or mid-air crises, some were more down to earth. On a more spiritual note, an Eastern Airlines pilot, O.A. Fish, found out that his wife was a "secret tongue speaker." One evening she persuaded him to watch Pat Robertson's 700 Club where he heard glossolalia for the first time. "The language sounded like Arabic or Hebrew to me," he explained, " and I could feel my hair standing up on the back of my neck." Later he received tongues himself while "a glory filled the room and a new language of praise gushed forth for almost an hour."[17]

Another pilot, Bruce Mansfield, while on a flight from Yakima, Washington to Redding, California, received the tongues experience while piloting a plane alone at 12,000 feet and going 200 miles an hour. He later said that "someone else was at the controls at the time." He landed safely.[18]

CONVERSIONS

Many testimonies gave witness to powerful conversions from atheism, agnosticism, the occult, and false religions. Many others told of conversions from mainline Protestant formality to Pentecostal fervor. A typical Protestant testimony was that of Frederick Savage, a United Methodist from Fairbanks, Alaska who was a self-described "Unitarian Methodist until I faced the moment of truth" and was converted from "social activism." He later was invited to speak in a church on how he received the baptism in the Holy Spirit "without tongues." On his way, however, he began to speak in tongues. He revised his talk and fulfilled the invitation anyway.[19]

A testimony by Masatoshi Yoshimura of Kyoto, Japan told of his conversion from Buddhism to Christianity after an FGBMFI airlift to the Far East in 1974. On a trip to the U.S. he attended the Full Gospel World Convention where he made a full surrender of his life to Christ. A high corporate leader in the Japanese Sanyo chemical company, Yoshimura became a leading Christian spokesman to his fellow Japanese. A similar testimony told of the conversion of Gary Archer of Sturgis, Michigan from Mormonism. This began in 1983 when he picked up a copy of Full Gospel Business Men's *Voice* in a fast food restaurant. Reading the magazine during a lunch break, he suddenly became disillusioned with the "works righteousness" of Mormonism. Later calling the Latter Day Saints a "cult," he joined a Pentecostal church, feeling as he said "clean...for the first time in years I was truly happy."[20]

BAPTISM IN THE HOLY SPIRIT AND TONGUES

Perhaps the most pertinent testimonies were those of people who were baptized in the Holy Spirit and spoke in tongues as the evidence of their Pentecostal experience. Almost every testimony published in *Voice* included this vital component. One of the earliest and most important Pentecostal testimonies ever to appear in *Voice* was that of the founder of the Neo-Pentecostal movement, Dennis Bennett, pastor of St. Mark's Episcopal Church in Van Nuys, California. Published in 1960, the article was published within months of Bennett's famous "Nine O'Clock in the Morning" experience. His testimony was:

> "When I prayed for God to grant me the fullness of the Spirit and opened my mouth to praise Him, I found to my amazement that as I repeated words of praise, the Holy Spirit did take my lips and tongue and form a new and powerful language of praise and prayer that I myself could not understand, and that as I so praised God, the Holy Spirit did fill me with joy and peace and power which has not departed!"[21]

Other testimonies told of instances of "zenoglossolalia," the extremely rare and miraculous utterance of tongues in a known earthly language, unknown to the speaker. At least three instances of this phenomenon were reported in *Voice,* one by no less a person than Demos Shakarian himself. The incident was reported by Donald Liedmann, a "converted Orthodox Jew" who was familiar with several middle eastern languages. At an FGBMFI meeting he reported that "I began to weep. Demos Shakarian was praying in a language he had never learned—ancient Aramaic—the language Jesus had spoken."[22]

In a regional FGBMFI convention in Phoenix on January 30, 1961, John P. Wildrianne, a native of Liege, Belgium, heard an American named Danny Henry give a message in tongues which sounded "French-like." To his astonishment, the person who interpreted, Anette Long, gave an interpretation that was " a wonderful message." The problem was that Henry did not know French, although Long, the interpreter was a native French speaker. Incredulous, Wildrianne approached Henry and the American began to pray for him in tongues. "I understood every word! It was French." Later Wildrianne was converted.[23]

Another case of reported zenoglossolalia involved Harald Bredesen while he served as pastor of the First Reformed Church of America in Mt. Vernon, New York. The *Daily Argus* newspaper reported that Bredesen had spoken in Polish, Arabic, Greek, various Slavic languages and even "ancient Egyptian." These utterances which were on audiotape, were later investigated by Eugene Nida of the American Bible Society and tentatively identified as Paul's "unknown tongue of I Corinthians." These incidents, it was reported, caused "surprised awe and uncomfortable consternation" in Bredesen's Reformed congregation.[24]

These testimonies, and countless others like them, were given in thousands of chapter meetings and conventions, were published by the hundreds in *Voice* and other FGBMFI publications, TV, radio, and were passed from hand to hand in the form of thousands of audiotapes. They constituted the heart and soul of the Fellowship and expressed its central focus. Testimonies were the voice of the common men who were touched by God. Often simple and lacking in theological precision, they nevertheless expressed better than anything else the mission and focus of FGBMFI.

1. See Tom Battle, "Face to Face," Voice, *May, 1991, pp. 2-10.*

2. George Morrison, "I've Got to Get Out," Voice, *September 198, pp. 30-34; Tim Janz, "Busted Back to God," Voice, November 1980, pp. 24-28.*

3. See Voice, *August, 1988, pp. 3-9.*

4. See Voice, *March, 1987, pp. 20-23.*

5. Ron Jesser, "Going Straight," Voice, *February 1982, pp. 10-15; Jim Johnson, "Beyond Rejection," Voice, December, 1986, pp. 30-34; Sy Rogers, "Trapped in the Wrong Body," Voice, June 1985, pp. 27-33; Cliff Dudley, "Three Lives," Voice, January, 1983, pp. 34-37; Jim Conway, "A Man in Mid- Life Crisis," Voice, November, 1988, pp. 16-23.*

6. Jim Ripley, "I Found the Answer," Voice, *June, 1973, p 29.*

7. Tom Landry, "Winning: Is it Most Important?" Voice, *November, 1986, pp. 2-10; Jim Ryun, "Fastest Man Alive," Voice, April 1983, pp. 6-38.*

8. See Voice, *January 1980, pp. 16-20 (Kyle Rote); September 1979, (Robert Birdsong); June 1981, pp. 26-29 (Besmanoff); August 1984, pp. 8-13 (David Story); June 1987, pp. 12-16 (Gene Burress) and January 1987, pp. 30-34 (Ed Dmitri).*

9. Harold Cole, "Never to Walk Again?" Voice, *June 1988, pp. 13-24.*

10. Mychal Thompson, "The Power of Priorities," Voice, *September, 1989, pp. 2-7.*

11. See "The Clown Prince," Voice, *July, 1984, pp. 4-9.*

12. Carl Lewis, "Reaching for the Gold," Voice, *October, 1988, pp. 3-6.*

13. Norman Williams, "Terror at Tenerife," Voice, *April 1979, pp. 2-6*

14. Frank Foglio, "Wings of Protection," Voice, *September 1975, pp. 16-20; Bill Stinson, "Was My Number Up?" Voice, October 1982, pp. 2-5, 30.*

15. Jerry L. Wilkins, "No Alternative," Voice, *December, 1976, pp. 18-32.*

16. Charles Carney, "Intervention of Another Kind," Voice, *June 1983, pp. 32- 38.*

17. Captain O.A. Fish, "On Course," Voice, *May 1981, pp. 17-19.*

18. See Voice, *February, 1974, p. 33.*

19. Frederick Savage, "The Moment of Truth," Voice, *June 1973, pp. 13-30.*

20. See Masatoshi Yoshimura, "The Quest," Voice, *June, 1974, pp. 2-7; Gary Archer, "Vain Striving," May 1987, pp. 22-27.*

21. Dennis J. Bennett, "They Spake in Tongues and Magnified God," Voice, *October, 1960, pp. 6-8.*

22. Donald Liedmann, "A New Covenant," *p. 11*

23. See "God Spoke to Me in French," Voice, *March 1961, pp. 3-8.*

24. Ruth Weber, "Speaking in Tongues Awes Dutch Reformed Church," Voice, *May 1961, pp. 12-13.*

Chapter Eleven

THE FELLOWSHIP AT FORTY

"God has shown me the future, and has revealed that a 'New Wave of Revival' is about to explode within the Body of Christ. The powerful miracle vision God gave me for the Fellowship and the world, is not over..."—Demos Shakarian, 1991

The dedication of the new headquarters in Costa Mesa in 1980 inaugurated a new decade full of promise for even greater things than anything yet seen in the history of the Fellowship. Around the world, reports of spectacular growth were sent in to the headquarters. *Voice* continued to grow in size and in quality as did the other non-English editions published by the Fellowship. The growth in overseas chapters was nothing short of phenomenal. As a case in point, the Australians, who could claim only six chapters in 1976, were able to report no less than 70 chapters in 1984. The United Kingdom alone reported 173 chapters in that year. In Latin America, growth was also pronounced. In 1984, Brazil claimed 25 chapters. This was encouraging growth indeed.[1]

To track the worldwide growth of the Fellowship, a "World Chapter Directory" was published in 1981 that showed the city, name, meeting time and place, the President along with his telephone number. The booklet listed 2,408 chapters around the world. The new directory was a convenient tracking service for those who might need help anywhere in the world. A case in point came in 1981 when a father in North Carolina needed someone to minister to a "wayward son" stranded in Oklahoma. A call to the local FGBMFI president not only located the son, but led to his conversion! The directory sold for $3.95.[2]

The 1983 convention which gathered in Detroit echoed the optimistic atmosphere that seemed to permeate the entire organization. Upwards of 15,000 people "received ministry" in this convention, including the 2,000 who were converted at the altar calls. Among these were 200 young people. Speakers who led in the convention included Kenneth Copeland, Kenneth Hagin, John Wimber, Roy Hicks, and John Osteen. These "faith" teachers gave the Fellowship a mentality to believe that all things were indeed possible to him who believed.[3]

The convention was told that in February of 1983, a new U.S. constitution was adopted "in the light of international growth." Furthermore, new goals were set by the Board of Directors. "A chapter in every nation," as well as 1,000,000 members in no less than 40,000 chapters worldwide. The goals were ambitious indeed, but past victories seemed to indicate that anything was possible for the future. To accelerate this anticipated growth, a new program was adopted in 1983 to train Full Gospel leaders for the future. Called "Super Advanced Leadership Training Seminars," were scheduled in 22 locations across America.[4]

Demos Shakarian continued to lead the Fellowship in the optimistic style that he had exuded since the founding days of the organization. Featured on the nationwide telecasts of the FGBMFI broadcast "Good News," he had become a familiar figure to millions of

Christians who tuned in to the television stations to pick up the program. In fact, in 1983, Demos, Steve Shakarian, executive producer, and Denny Ermel, producer/director were given awards by the Southern California Motion Picture Council for their outstanding contribution to the television industry.[5]

Shakarian, although entering his 70's continued to lead in his usual vigorous and apostolic fashion. Rather than contemplating retirement, he was always ready to "refire" and plan for the next convention. New prophecies continued to motivate him toward ever greater things. A typical prophecy was one given to Demos in 1978 in Turlock, California and published in *Voice* magazine under the title "Refired—Not Retired!"

> "The things that He has laid upon your heart have not yet fully come to pass...but My son, the hour is at hand when you shall have the fullness and the completeness...and it shall bless the nations."[6]

The momentum of the Fellowship during the 1980's continued to bring stories of new and exciting breakthroughs in unexpected places. An exotic report out of Southern California in 1983 told of the South Bay Regional dinner being held in the grand ballroom of the ocean liner Queen Mary which was docked in Long Beach. The "full and overflowing" crowd saw 25 conversions after a talk by the unique speaker, Sir Lionel Luckhoo, who had recently been knighted by Queen Elizabeth.[7]

With the Fellowship breaking new growth records, and with the national telecast reaching almost every home in America, few could have imagined that the greatest crisis ever faced by the Fellowship lurked just around the corner. The crisis began on March 3, 1984 when Shakarian was suddenly stricken with a massive stroke that temporarily left him incapacitated.

Needless to say, this event sent shock waves through the Fellowship as members around the world faced up to the possibility that new leadership might soon be necessary.[8]

A PROBLEM OF SUCCESSION

The glittering success of the Fellowship, symbolized by the new headquarters in Costa Mesa, masked a serious problem of leadership that, brought to the surface by the stroke, in a few years threatened to destroy the very existence of the organization. From the beginning, Demos Shakarian had played an indispensable role in founding and leading the Fellowship. His vision and example was the paradigm that fueled the growth of the movement. All along, he had attracted men of great vision and organizational ability who had brought Full Gospel chapters to most of the nations of the world. From the beginning, Shakarian served without salary, as did all the International Directors, who by 1988 numbered 150 men.[9]

Few members worried about the future of the Fellowship as long as the president remained in good health. The stroke severely hampered his activities for many months. To help the ailing leader, the Executive Vice President, Thomas Ashcraft, a long-time International Director from Texas, was called to serve as acting president until Shakarian could recover. Soon Ashcraft and other top leaders including Vice-Presidents Norman Norwood and Secretary Lynwood Maddox, as well as Treasurer Gerald Walker, agreed that Shakarian was incapable of continuing to give the necessary vision and leadership needed for the future.[10]

Another concern of the leadership was the fact that in 1983, the membership of the Fellowship in the United States began to level off. In 1984 there was an actual decline in U.S. membership although the number of chapters increased slightly.[11]

A severe crisis broke out in 1987 when three International Directors, Ashcraft, Norwood and Maddox, requested that Shakarian "retire and become Chairman of the Board," Norwood explained he would be president. When presented with the idea of stepping down, Demos said, "I want to pray about it, and talk to the other Directors." He refused to do it. "God won't let me do it," he explained. Within a few months Tommy Ashcraft had passed away and Norman Norwood became "Executive Vice-President."[12]

Norwood, along with Lynwood Maddox and others, charged Shakarian with "irregularities" in reporting and charging his travel expenses. A preliminary "review" of the Fellowship's financial records, which were withheld from Shakarian, led to a decision to remove him from active leadership while allowing him to remain as a figurehead "Spiritual Director." The day-to-day operation of the Fellowship was then taken over by Norwood and a group of his supporters on the Board of Directors. This action Shakarian denounced as "trickery."[13]

Although much of the struggle for power occurred behind closed doors, enough news filtered down to the local chapters to cause serious losses in membership and support. Within two years, there was a reported drop in U.S. membership from 40,000 to 30,000 men. Through the entire episode, Shakarian maintained his complete innocence of all charges against him.[14]

THE SHAKARIAN RESTORATION

Again, a timely prophecy brought Shakarian back from the edge of discouragement and defeat, lifted his spirits and led him to once again overcome his prob-

lems. In October, 1987, during the time of his exile
from leadership, he visited the Eagle's Nest, a church in
nearby Newport Beach, California, pastored by Gary
Greenwald where four young pastors prayed for him.
In the middle of the prayer, one man prophesied:

> "I see a huge field, a green pasture, and you are
> sitting right in the middle of it. And I see locusts
> eating the green grass, eating real fast. They
> came right up to where you were sitting in a
> straight line. You were right on the edge of it.
> And the Lord was displeased with what was
> happening, so He gave one huge blast...Then
> the Lord said to you, "Stand tall. I'm going to
> give you new ideas, new directions, a whole
> bunch of wonderful new things. This work is
> not finished, so much more is going to be
> done."[15]

Armed with this prophecy and as resourceful as
ever, Shakarian soon mounted a counter attack. Three
of the men who assisted Demos in his counter-attack
were Gene Scalf, who presented the Shakarian side of
things to the men of the Fellowship; Attorney Terry
Steinhart, whose legal assistance was invaluable in pre-
paring the Shakarians' position, and Mark Bellinger
who made the presentation of Demos' defense to the
Board of Directors. At a Directors' meeting in Toronto
in 1988 Gene M. Ellerbee, a strong Shakarian supporter,
was elected as "Executive Vice-President" to help Shakarian in administering the affairs of the Fellowship.
The climactic meeting occurred in Nashville, Tennessee
in 1989 where the delegates removed seven
"rebellious" members of the Board of Directors who
were voted out of office.[16]

Demos Shakarian was successful in warding off
this, the most serious threat to his power since the
founding of the organization. A subsequent accounting

of the financial records cleared Shakarian of the charges of not reporting his travel expenses. But he and the Fellowship paid a heavy price for their victory. According to Jerry Jensen, editor of *Voice* magazine and public spokesman for Shakarian during the entire affair, "*Voice* and everything we did was cut in half. That included employees at headquarters, the number of chapters in the United States, and the financial income at headquarters."[17]

Despite these setbacks, the Fellowship continued to grow, especially outside the United States. Even during the dark days of division, the reports from the world conventions were positive and upbeat. Visitors to the 1987 World Convention in Anaheim might have never known that anything was amiss to judge from the reports of the sessions which were attended by 8,000 people. Speakers such as Kenneth Hagin, Pat Robertson, Gene M. Ellerbee, and Father Ralph Di Orio spoke of "a new wave of renewal" and a "fresh approach to world evangelism." One notable exception was the occasion when Kenneth Hagin stopped in the middle of his message and turned and addressed the Board Members on the platform accusing them of failing to respond to the leading of the Holy Spirit.[18]

THE FELLOWSHIP AT FORTY

At the beginning of the decade of the 1990's the irrepressible Shakarian was again in complete control of the FGBMFI organization writing books with titles such as *A New Wave of Revival: The Vision Intensified.* With Gene M. Ellerbee at his side to help with the day-to-day business of the organization, Shakarian and the reconstituted Board looked forward to the fortieth anniversary celebration of the Fellowship to begin in San Francisco in 1992.[19]

Even after years of division and reorganization, FGBMFI still represented a formidable spiritual force in America and the world. Indicative of better things to come, by the end of 1991, the overall growth of the Fellowship is increasing once again.

The steady growth of chapters and membership overseas, moreover, indicated that the major problems experienced by the Fellowship were confined mostly to the United States and were not exported outside the country.

A NEW WAVE

In 1991, the World Convention in Orlando elected Richard Shakarian, oldest son of Demos and Rose Shakarian as an International Vice-President of the Fellowship. In 1990, Demos had been invited to minister in Armenia where he is something of a national hero, representing an Armenian family that made a success in America. Since Demos could not make the trip because of health reasons, he sent his son Richard to speak in his place. While in Yerevan, the capital of Armenia, he preached to crowds of up to 15,000 persons. While there he organized the first Armenian chapter of FGBMFI. By 1992, the number of Armenian chapters had grown to ten.[20]

The Armenian ministry of Richard brought to full circle the story of the Armenian connection with the American Pentecostal movement at the turn of the century. With the fall of European communism, the door was now open for FGBMFI, along with other Christian churches and movements, to bring a revival of New Testament Christianity to Armenia and other East European nations that were cut off by the "Iron Curtain" for most of the century.[21]

Indeed, as the fellowship looked forward to new

waves of revival in the future, Demos Shakarian often looked back to the early days of the Fellowship for fresh inspiration. In an impassioned *Voice* article in 1986 he had admonished:

> "We must get back to the old-fashioned way. The old-fashioned way of praying; the old-fashioned way of ballroom meetings; back to the vision which birthed this Fellowship—to reach the world with the message of the baptism in the Holy Spirit, the message of healing, and the demonstration of the supernatural power of God in action."[22]

When the 1991 World Convention convened in Orlando, as he had done so often before, Demos invited Oral Roberts to be the main speaker. Again Roberts accepted, but with one proviso, that they hold their sessions in the ballroom of the hotel and not in the convention center. He counseled the businessmen "Don't get away from your call. Don't try to be a religious organization. Be business and professional people that do not know a lot about theology...major on your testimony." In other words, continue to be "God's Ballroom Saints." Sure enough, the convention was held in the ballroom of the Orlando Peabody Hotel while the convention center was empty across the street. FGBMFI was back home again, just as they began in Clifton's Cafeteria forty years before in 1951, in a dining room with Demos in charge and Oral Roberts as the main speaker.[23]

EPILOGUE

Despite the twin problems of succession and schism, Full Gospel Business Men's Fellowship International approached the end of its fourth decade with a remarkable record of accomplishments. Beginning on the crest of the healing/deliverance crusades of William Branham, Oral Roberts, and Tommy Hicks, the Fellowship helped to bring Pentecostalism into previously unknown territories. The appeal to the middle classes of businessmen and professionals helped break the stereotype of the poor, uneducated sectarian Pentecostal that had been familiar to most Americans.

The openness of the Fellowship to the charismatic renewal in the mainline churches after 1960 also created a historic role for FGBMFI as the chapters and conventions became major platforms for early leaders from all the churches including the Roman Catholics. Furthermore, FGBMFI's *Voice* became the major publication of record for several years to those whose testimonies fueled the renewal both in America and in other nations.

Without these "Pentecostal Merchants" of salvation, to borrow a phrase from Steve Durasoff, it is doubtful if the charismatic movement would have developed as broadly as it did, or as fast as it did. In fact, in 1945 all the Pentecostals in the world numbered only 16 million persons. By 1992, that figure had ballooned to 411 million people making up about 25% of all the Christians in the world. A large part of that growth could be credited to the efforts of Full Gospel Business Men's Fellowship International. And, despite all obstacles, Demos Shakarian was able to rejoice as his organization of Spirit-filled businessmen became a major force in the religious world of the twentieth century.[24]

1. *See "Encouraging Growth Noted,"* Voice, *May 1984, p. 25.*

2. *See* Voice, *September, 1981, p. 17.*

3. *See "Detroit '83,"* Voice, *September, 1983, pp. 19-25.*

4. Ibid. *See "Update! Super Advanced Leadership Training Seminars,"* Voice, *February, 1985, p.31.*

5. Voice, *July/August, 1983, "Chief Operating Officer," p. 7.*

6. *"Refired—Not Retired,"* Voice, *May 1978, p. 23.*

7. *See "South Bay Regional Banquet,"* Voice, *June, 1983, p. 15.*

8. *The story of the stroke was given by Shakarian at the commencement of Oral Roberts University in 1984 where he was given a Doctor of Laws degree by Roberts. See "Pruned to Profit,"* Voice, *September, 1984, pp. 34-36. Also see* Voice, *March 1985, p. 19.*

9. *From the beginning, the independently wealthy Shakarian had refused to accept a salary, although the Fellowship paid his travel, meal and hotel expenses while traveling on the business of the organization. Shakarian-Synan interview, February 2, 1988, pp. 20-25.*

10. Ibid., *Jerry Jensen, personal Interview with the author, April 12, 1991.*

11. *See Steve Shakarian, "Organizational Assessment," p. 4.*

12. *Synan-Shakarian interview; Synan-Jensen interview.*

13. *Shakarian-Synan interview,* Ibid., *also see "FGBMFI Struggles Toward the Future,"* Charisma, *March, 1988, p. 24.*

14. *Shakarian-Synan interview,* Ibid.

15. *This prophecy was recounted during an interview with Shakarian by the author on October 5, 1987 at his home in Downey, California. As he recalled it, the church was called the Eagle's Nest under a pastor Greenwald.*

16. *For a review of developments to 1989, see: "Full Gospel Fellowship Restores Shakarian, Board Clears Founder and President of Mishandling Funds Charges,"* Charisma, *March 1989, p. 32.*

17. *Jerry Jensen, interview with the author. February 15, 1992, Costa Mesa, California.*

18. *See* Voice, *August, 1987, p. 15.*

19. *Demos Shakarian,* A New Wave of Revival; The Vision Intensifies *(Costa Mesa, CA; FGBMFI, N.D.).*

20. *Interview with Richard Shakarian, May 27, 1992.*

21. *Richard Shakarian, "A Real Breakthrough,"* Voice, *(European edition), May/June, p. 2-14.*

22. *Demos Shakarian, "Focus on Healing,"* Voice, *January, 1986, pp. 2-30.*

23. *Oral Roberts interview, pp. 33-34.*

24. *See David Barrett,* World Christian Encyclopedia *(London; Oxford*

University Press, 1982). Also see his follow-up survey on the Pentecostal /Charismatic Movement, "Global Statistics" in Burgess, et. al, Dictionary of Pentecostal and Charismatic Movements, *pp. 810-830.*

APPENDIX

OUR VISION

Our vision for the Fellowship is based upon a series of prophetic messages given over a period of time and conFIrmed by a literal vision from God.

In the vision, untold masses of men from every continent and nation, of all races and diverse culture and costume, once spiritually dead, are now alive. Delivered and set free, they are filled with the power of God's Holy Spirit, faces radiant with glory, hands raised and voices lifting their praises to heaven.

We see a vast global movement of laymen being used mightily by God to bring in this last great harvest through the outpouring of God's Holy Spirit before the return of our Lord Jesus Christ.

OUR MISSION

To reach men in all nations for Jesus Christ.
To train and equip men to fulfill the Great Commission.
To help believers to be baptized in the Holy Spirit and to grow spiritually.
To call men back to God.
To provide an opportunity for Christian Fellowship.
To bring a greater unity among all people in the body of Christ.

INTERNATIONAL CABINET

Demos Shakarian, President, (714) 754-1400
Gene M. Ellerbee, Executive Vice President,
(714) 754-1400
John Carrett, Vice President, 011-502-251-0432
Kwabena Darko, Vice President,
011-233-21-774-902
Dr. Douglas Fowler, Jr., Vice President
(912) 758-3313
Bernie Gray, Vice President, 011-61-7-397-3557
Khoo Oon Theam, Vice President,
011-65-225-3964
Col. Hank Lackey, Secretary, (513) 426-5123
Ralph Marinacci, Vice President, (904) 234-6223
James McEwan, Vice President, (416) 432-8088
Carlin W. Nash, Vice President, (401) 783-5737
Don L. Ostrom, Vice President, (206) 641-1400
Bill Phipps, Vice President, (816) 333-7738
Custodio R. Pires, Vice President,
011-55-21-711-7505
James M. Rogers, Vice President, (404) 476-4088
Richard Shakarian, Vice President,
(714) 662-1234
Ronny Svenhard, Treasurer, (510) 834-5035
James R. Winter, Vice President,
011-44-50587-3618

USA DISTRICT VICE PRESIDENTS

North Pacific, Mel Tombre, (406) 776-2206, res.
South Pacific, Ronny Svenhard,
(510) 834-5035, bus.
Mountain, Clem Dixon, (505) 822-8154, res.
West North Central, Bill Phipps, (816) 333-7738
Appalachian, Bill Cooke, (614) 861-3979, res.

Coastal Atlantic, Hoyt Elliott, (615) 292-0349, res.
South Atlantic, Jimmy Rogers,
(404) 476-4088, res.
New England, Carlin Nash, (401) 783-5737, res.

FGBMFI WORLD HEADQUARTERS

3150 Bear Street / Costa Mesa, CA 92626
(714) 754-1400

FGBMFI REGIONAL OFFICES

AFRICA REGIONAL OFFICE
Phone: 011-233-51-3740, 011-233-51-5934,
Fax: 011-233-51-6126
ASIA REGIONAL OFFICE
Phone: 011-65-224-9255, Fax: 011-65-223-4529
CANADA REGIONAL OFFICE
Phone: 1-416-675-1717, Fax: 1-416-675-1718
EUROPE REGIONAL OFFICE
Phone: 011-32-16-20-7944, Fax: 011-32-16-20-7931
LATIN AMERICA/CARIBBEAN REGIONAL OFFICE
Phone: 011-502-2-535991, Fax: 011-502-2-26402
MIDDLE EAST REGIONAL OFFICE
Phone: 011-44-63-611825, Fax: 011-44-50-865115
SOUTH AMERICA REGIONAL OFFICE
Phone: 011-55-21-719-8228, Fax: 011-55-21-701-6473
SOUTH PACIFIC REGIONAL OFFICE
Phone: 011-61-7-397-3557, 011-61-7-397-3130
Fax: 011-61-7-394-1049

FGBMFI NATIONAL OFFICES

Antigua & Barboda National Office
Phone: 1-809-462-3993, Fax: 1-809-462-1187

Argentina National Office
Phone: 011-54-1-943-4375, Fax: 011-54-1-91-4375
Australia National Office
Phone: 011-61-7-397-3557, Fax: 011-61-7-394-1049
Bahamas National Office
Phone: 1-809-325-6039
Barbados National Office
Phone: 1-809-436-8936, Fax: 1-809-429-8792
Belgium National Office
Phone: 011-32-16-20-7944, Fax: 011-32-16-20-7931
Belize National Office
Phone: 011-501-2-45042, Fax: 011-501-2-45979
Benin National Office
Phone: 011-229-31-53-90
Brazil National Office
Fax: 011-55-21-701-6473
British Virgin Islands National Office
Phone: 1-809-494-3843
Burkina Faso National Office
Phone: 011-226-31-21-41, 011-226-33-42-93
Burundi National Office
Phone: 011-257-24-01-18
Caribbean Area National Office
Phone: 1-809-949-7790, Fax: 1-809-949-9086
Cayman Islands National Office
Phone: 1-809-949-4090, Fax: 1-809-949-4090
Central African Republic National Office
Phone: 011-236-61-54-46
Congo National Office
Phone: 011-242-83-04-39
Costa Rica National Office
Phone: 011-506-27-5412, Fax: 011-506-27-0409
Cyprus National Office
Phone: 011-357-2-453983
Denmark National Office
Phone: 011-45-1-629-292

Dominica National Office
Phone: 1-809-448-2321
Dominican National Office
Phone: 1-809-566-5811
Egypt National Office
Phone: 011-20-2-340-3588
El Salvador National Office
Phone: 011-503-251-747, 011-503-284-295
Fax: 011-503-272-985
Fiji National Office
Phone: 011-679-30-1301, Fax: 011-679-30-0674
Finland National Office
Fax: 011-3-58-032-0715
France National Office
Phone: 011-33-14-637-4246
Gabon National Office
Phone: 011-241-73-20-00
Gambia National Office
Phone: 011-220-95107
Germany National Office
Fax: 011-49-91-147-6480
Ghana National Office
Phone: 011-233-21-22-57-55
Grenada National Office
Phone: 1-809-440-3061, Fax: 1-809-440-3890
Guadeloupe National Office
Phone: 011-590-26-8092, 011-590-26-8641
Guatemala National Office
Phone: 011-502-2-366-427, 011-502-2-372-122
Fax: 011-502-2-347-275
Guinea National Office
Phone: 011-224-4-46-51-41
Honduras National Office
Phone: 011-504-524-812, 011-504-224-008
Hong Kong National Office
Phone: 011-852-0-493-1830, Fax: 011-852-0-415-8568

India National Office
Phone: 011-91-22-642-0266
Indonesia National Office
Phone: 011-62-21-649-8623, Fax: 011-62-21-649-9556
Israel National Office
Phone: 011-972-2-240-572
Ivory Coast National Office
Phone: 011-225-41-40-41, 011-225-41-54-07
Jamaica National Office
Phone: 1-809-927-6794, Fax: 1-809-978-1347
Japan National Office
Phone: 011-81-298-22-3698, Fax: 011-81-298-22-3357
Kenya National Office
Phone: 011-254-2-33-39-40, 011-254-2-22-29-29
Fax: 011-254-2-72-89-49
Malaysia National Office
Phone: 011-60-3-241-1731, 011-60-3-241-1962
Fax: 011-60-3-248-9152
Malta National Office
Phone: 011-356-692-266
Martinique National Office
Phone: 011-596-51-2164, Fax: 011-596-50-5185
Mexico National Office
Phone: 011-52-8-335-3535 ext. 2172,
Fax: 011-52-83-358135
Montserrat National Office
Phone: 1-809-491-6252
Netherlands National Office
Phone: 011-31-70-863-263
Netherlands Antilles National Office
Phone: 011-599-967-2321, Fax: 011-599-967-6000
New Zealand National Office
Phone: 011-64-9-444-9478, Fax: 011-64-9-443-1063
Nicaragua National Office
Phone: 011-505-311-4440, 011-505-311-2143

Nigeria National Office
Phone: 011-234-84-33-56-59
Norway National Office
Phone: 011-47-34-88567
Papua New Guinea National Office
Phone: 011-675-42-4344, Fax: 011-675-42-2892
Paraguay National Office
Phone: 011-595-21-495-558, Fax: 011-595-21-448-145
Peru National Office
Phone: 011-51-14-715549, 011-51-14-717520
Fax: 011-51-14-338626
Philippines National Office
Phone: 011-63-2-832-5413, Fax: 011-63-2-833-5689
Romania National Office
Phone: 011-40-0-30-89-61
Rwanda National Office
Phone: 011-250-72216, 011-250-72316
Senegal National Office
Phone: 011-221-23-09-82, 011-221-22-28-20
Sierra Leone National Office
Phone: 011-232-22-23952, 011-232-22-31805
Singapore National Office
Phone: 011-65-223-4529, Fax: 011-65-223-4529
South Africa National Office
Phone: 011-27-12-330-1330, Fax: 011-27-12-546-0656
St. Christopher & Nevis National Office
Phone: 1-809-452-4880
Sweden National Office
Phone: 011-46-32-080-435
Taiwan National Office
Phone: 011-886-2-397-1233, Fax: 011-886-2-397-1230
Tanzania National Office
Phone: 011-255-57-051-2521
Thailand National Office
Phone: 011-66-2-250-0185, Fax: 011-66-2-251-5745

Togo National Office
Phone: 011-228-21-61436, 011-228-21-7688
Fax: 011-228-21-6236
Trinidad & Tobago National Office
Phone: 1-809-652-2543, Fax: 1-809-652-2253
Uganda National Office
Phone: 011-256-41-23-15-73, 011-256-41-26-77-55
United Kingdom National Office
Phone: 011-44-565-632-667, Fax: 011-44-565-755-639
Zaire National Office
Phone: 011-243-12-25462, Fax: 011-243-12-23623
Zambia National Office
Phone: 011-260-1-21-11-89
Zimbabwe National Office
Phone: 011-263-4-36-26-78